160401

NICHOLAS STERN

A STRATEGY
FOR
DEVELOPMENT

THE WORLD BANK
Washington, D.C.

Contents

Preface

This is a time when many are asking questions about the functioning of the world economy and the involvement of poor people in economic growth and development. The meaning of development is itself under scrutiny. Underlying the questioning are profound changes in the world economy over the last 20 years. These include: strong advances in economic policy and growth in many developing countries, most strikingly in the two population giants, China and India; declining living standards in many other developing countries; devastating civil conflicts, particularly in Africa; the collapse of the former Soviet bloc, with a transition to a market economy that has been traumatic for many; huge increases in private capital flows; the rise of information technology and the Internet; and the rapid spread of AIDS. Less noticed, but equally profound, the last two decades of the twentieth century coincided with a deepening understanding of the meaning of development and the first strong and sustained reduction in the proportion of people living in poverty for around 200 years.

These changes, the questioning, and the advance of our understanding together provide an opportunity and a challenge to the international development community. We have an opportunity to "raise our game" in the fight against poverty and, working together, with greater resources and better policies to make real progress in reducing poverty. To meet this challenge, it is important to have a coherent intellectual approach to development to guide our actions and to ensure that our work really does include poor people.

During his first year as Chief Economist and Senior Vice President of the World Bank, Nick Stern articulated the outlines of an emerging strategy for development in a series of speeches during visits to our clients, including several of the world's most populous developing countries. His remarks draw upon the growing body of knowledge in development economics, the research and operational experience of the Bank, and his own varied experience as an economist, including the eight months he spent as a young researcher in an impoverished village in India.

The speeches represent Nick's own views, in the sense that they have not been cleared or endorsed by the World Bank executive directors.

I am certain that this small collection will become an important part of the development literature. We are at an exciting and challenging moment as we approach the future growth of our planet, and I commend this work to you for your review and consideration.

James D. Wolfensohn

Introduction

As this volume was going to press, hijacked jetliners destroyed New York's World Trade Center and a portion of the Pentagon in Washington, D.C. It is a time of grief. It is a time for reflection. For me, as for many others of my generation, the magnitude of the tragedy and the anxiety about events that will follow recall the challenges that confronted our parents, the generation that came of age during the Second World War.

The survivors of that terrible conflagration rededicated themselves to international dialogue and cooperation, so that future generations might be spared the immense suffering of global war. They created new organizations: the United Nations, to foster political dialogue and cooperation, and the World Bank and the International Monetary Fund, to provide the economic basis for a lasting peace. Europeans established the European Coal and Steel Community, the drab institutional foundation of what has become the European Union. The goal was to build a world of cohesion and inclusion in place of conflict and inequality. It was an affirmation of our common humanity.

The institutions they created are far from perfect, and the protection against war that they have afforded has been very far from complete. Wars and even genocides have continued to occur, despite the heartfelt pledges of "never again." Notwithstanding unprecedented success in reducing poverty and extending the benefits of health care and education, almost three billion of the world's six billion people live on less than two dollars a day.

Yet the efforts to create a more equitable and peaceful world have not been in vain. Less than a generation ago, the risk of nuclear war among the large industrialized nations imperiled the very continuation of life on earth. Today that threat has receded. The international community has also intervened—albeit inconsistently—to end local conflicts, to halt genocide, and to administer justice to criminals who flout international codes for civilized behavior whether it be in the name of nationalism or ideology or any other reason. In the past decade, improved policies and institutions in poor countries, more effective development assistance, and a more open international environment for trade and investment have made possible the most rapid reduction in poverty seen in human history. Since 1980 the overall number of poor people has stopped increasing, and has indeed fallen by an estimated 200 million (figure 1).

Working together to fight poverty can help reduce conflict in two ways. The act of working together for a higher goal should be a constant reminder of our common humanity and a shared world. And, still more important, a more inclusive world, a more equitable world, one of mutual respect and collaboration between different nations, cultures and faiths will surely be a world where the hatred that fuels terrorism and conflict is much less likely to fester.

The lessons of World War II, and the successes and failures of multilateral cooperation and international development efforts since then, surely provide a valuable guide for how to proceed. First, international problems require an international response. Second, ideas and knowledge are crucial to finding better responses. As the international community has learned more about development—what works, what does not and why—developing country governments and donors have been able to craft better policies and institutions and thus to make better use of available resources in the fight against poverty.

I believe we are already seeing a renewed commitment to three ideas that recur throughout this volume: the importance of having effective international institutions to address international problems, the value of knowledge, and above all the importance of the fight against poverty and inequity to build a better world.

About This Volume

The speeches in this collection—all delivered since I became chief economist of the World Bank in July 2000—reflect insights gained over more than three decades of study and work in development economics. Together they attempt to provide an analysis of development experience and an agenda for action in the coming years. This introductory essay is intended to set the evolution of my own ideas within the context of the changes in development thinking and strategy that I have seen take place.

We are all strongly influenced by our intellectual predecessors and colleagues, and I have drawn on many strands of research in economic theory and development economics. Readers will recognize, in particular, the influence of the work of Joseph Schumpeter, Albert Hirschman, and Amartya Sen. Since arriving in the Bank, I have been strongly influenced by working closely with James Wolfensohn, the President of the World Bank.

My colleagues in the Development Economics Vice Presidency (DEC) have played a central role in the development of the ideas in these speeches and the speeches themselves. Paul Collier and David Dollar are co-authors of Chapter 2. Shahrokh Fardoust was central to Chapter 3 on India and Chapter 5 on Pakistan. David Dollar and David Ellerman worked closely with me on the chapter on China, and David Ellerman played a key role in Chapters 7 and 8. Coralie Gevers, Ian Goldin, and Jo Ritzen have contributed to several chapters. Many other colleagues, both in DEC and in other parts of the Bank, have contributed in important ways, and I hope they will accept my collective thanks. Halsey Rogers helped with the creation and crafting of the speeches throughout the year and guided the editing of this collection to reduce repetition. I owe him a great debt. I am very grateful to Lawrence MacDonald for encouraging me to explain these ideas in the context of my own experience. I am also grateful to Nancy Levine for editing the manuscript, and to Heather Worley and the Office of the Publisher at the World Bank for turning the manuscript into a book.

Notwithstanding the great support from my colleagues at the World Bank, I must emphasize strongly that the views expressed here are my own and not those of the World Bank.

Development Thinking: From Planning to Market Fundamentalism

The 1960s, the period during which I came of age as an economist, was still an era of confident, ambitious government. Around the world, both the general public and public officials believed that government could understand the economy well and lead it strongly in certain directions. This belief had a variety of political expressions, from the activist domestic policies of the Kennedy and Johnson administrations in the United States to the social democratic and interventionist policies in Western Europe that were endorsed even by conservatives like de Gaulle. And throughout the developing world, the 1960s was an era when central planning, or at least the idea of central planning, was in the ascendancy. The belief that government action could overcome most market failures was widely accepted not only in the eastern bloc economies and China but also in India and the newly independent states of Africa. In short, idealistic views of government reigned, even in societies as historically skeptical as the United States. This idealism stemmed in no small part from what was seen as government's successful role in fighting fascism and ending economic depression in earlier decades.

The belief in the possibilities of government action was reflected as well in the economics we did—both the theoretical economics and the policy work. On the question of how best to manage the domestic economy, micro-theoretical models emphasized externalities and other market failures that limited the ability of markets to respond on their own and on the macro front the models highlighted Keynesian failures of effective demand and thus Keynes approaches to managing economic aggregates. Empirically, planning models still figured prominently, with India leading the way. As for the external economy, both theoretical and policy-oriented work expressed a suspicion of global markets that paralleled the questioning of the efficacy of domestic markets. Skeptics about what would later be called globalization, led by Raúl Prebisch and his colleagues at the UN Economic Commission for Latin America, highlighted the potential costs of opening borders to global competition, especially in the case of poorer countries that had not yet managed to establish an industrial base. This research both fed and reflected the movement toward import-substituting industrialization in much of the developing world—the rapid growth of such Latin American economies as Brazil's and Mexico's seemed to validate this approach.

Confidence in the ability of an activist government to improve welfare, whether through prescriptive plans for the development of the domestic economy, or through barriers to external trade, or Keynesian demand management, would break down over the ensuing two decades. Economic theory turned to causes of government failure, such as rent-seeking and rational expectations. Even the planning literature, with its benign view of government, began to tackle the incentive problems that plagued planning, which had eliminated any real role for prices. Most notably, the Diamond-Mirlees model attempted to bring the price mechanism into the planning story in a systematic way, in effect creating an integration of plan and market.

On the empirical side, evidence mounted that government failure was indeed important in the developing world. Central planning was undermined both by its colossal failures (white-elephant projects for which there turned out to be no demand) and by the smaller day-to-day disturbances and wastefulness that stemmed from the lack of price signals. And although import substitution contributed to impressive growth in some countries, support for that approach waned as its costs in terms of rent-seeking and difficulty competing in international markets became more and more apparent. India's experience amply illustrated both points. Macroeconomic stability and basic entrepreneurship kept the Indian economy growing, but the inefficiencies induced by planning and by the lack of foreign competition held back both growth and poverty reduction.

With the collapse of naïve confidence in government came an excessive, and equally naïve, confidence in the market, a reaction which swept across many industrial countries and received a great boost with the collapse of the Soviet bloc at the end of the 1980s. It also made great inroads in the developing world, where the potential for damage was far greater. In a number of public lectures and articles, I tried at the end of the 1980s and the beginning of the 1990s to warn against the simplified acceptance of a standard market-driven approach to policy. It would take another decade or two to build a viable and constructive new synthesis, one that would better define government's essential, but necessarily circumscribed, role in economic development.

Learning on the Ground: Small-Scale Tea Planting in Kenya

My own journey through this landscape of development was driven by experience in the field—beginning in the tea gardens of smallholders in Kenya and continuing in the wheatfields of India. One might ask why someone who had trained as a mathematical economist would have been tramping around in the fields. The answer is found in the belief in the power of policy, based on sound theory and serious evidence, to improve lives. Like other theorists of my generation, I headed south with a conviction that good economic policy would bring high returns in the hopeful but desperately poor countries of Africa and Asia.

My first foray into practical development economics took me to Kenya in 1969, where I carried out the fieldwork that led to an extensive study of the Kenyan Tea Development Authority. The KTDA was an innovative effort to help smallholders grow, process, and export tea, and it was carried out with great success over a number of years. It was founded on the efforts of the small farmers, primarily women, who did the hands-on work of growing and harvesting tea. Tea is a crop that requires close attention. The plants do not provide a good yield until four years after planting, and they reach full maturity only in seven or eight years. Quality is made in the field, and it can be easily destroyed if the tea is not transported to the factory quickly and carefully. For these reasons, tea is generally thought to be an estate crop. Nevertheless, in Kenya the skill and learning of the farmers made possible a smallholder-based model.

But for the model to work, coordination between the smallholders, the larger-scale private sector, and the state was needed. The government provided agricultural extension to help train the farmers, and it also had to furnish infrastructure, including good roads. (Tea grows only in wet conditions, but those same conditions are disastrous for the kind of dirt roads usually found in rural areas.) The third party, the larger-scale private sector, processed and marketed the tea.

The KTDA experience foreshadowed lessons that would recur often in my later work. First, successful development requires both a dynamic private sector and an active and efficient public sector. The public sector provides, when it operates well, the appropriate climate for investment (including promoting or providing infrastructure). Such a climate encourages collective action and breeds trust among market participants. Second, "private sector" means not just multinationals and large domestic firms but also small businesses and microenterprises. Poor people, including small farmers, have great capacity to power economic growth; all they need, typically, is a hand to get started, an absence of bureaucratic harassment, and a few tools to allow them to participate in growth. Third, when combined with a good investment climate, integration with the world economy—in this case, global tea markets—can expand possibilities and hasten development.

Looking back, the KTDA package appears even richer than it did three decades ago. But it is not an easy package to pull together, and it can unravel for many reasons—for example, if payments to farmers are unreliable or if the public authority becomes inefficient or corrupt. Indeed, more recent Kenyan history has not been kind to the KTDA, as governance worsened and the state upset the balance of the public-private partnership.

Learning on the Ground: An Indian Village

Soon after my time in Kenya, I began in 1974 a lifelong relationship with the village of Palanpur in the state of Uttar Pradesh, India. Together with Christopher Bliss, I spent eight months living in the village and collecting data on living standards. From a methodological perspective, this experience reinforced my deep belief in the importance of good data, but it also demonstrated that collecting such data is not an easy task. It was clear that no one-shot household survey could capture accurately the varied and dynamic experience of poor communities. Quantitative analysis must be accompanied by in-depth qualitative understanding of just what the data mean, lest they be misinterpreted or given too much weight.

Substantively, my experiences in Palanpur corroborated the policy lessons of Kenya, but largely in a negative way. Perhaps the clearest lesson was that just as a thoughtful and efficient government can promote private sector development even in poor regions, an overly interventionist, unresponsive, and inefficient state can shackle, or at least divert, the dynamism of small entrepreneurs and the energies of poor people.

In the terms that I will use extensively throughout this book, rural India in the 1970s lacked both of the key pillars of development: an investment climate conducive to growth and productivity, and policies and institutions that empower poor people to participate in development. True, it had the macroeconomic stability that is the first element in a good investment climate. But India's investment climate was deficient in most of the other ingredients: competition, a responsive government bureaucracy, good rural infrastructure, and a predictable and efficient legal system. In this environment, rural India unsurprisingly showed none of the dynamic off-farm private sector activity that is usually essential to successful rural development.

Furthermore, the people of Palanpur and similar villages lacked most of the tools necessary to participate in growth. Education and health care were thoroughly inadequate, and poor people and other disadvantaged groups were treated with disdain both by wealthier people and by the authorities. Their problems were compounded by pervasive discrimination against women and the lower castes—discrimination that the state did nothing effective to discourage. Not surprisingly, progress against poverty was very slow during the first decade of my association with Palanpur.

In both Kenya and Palanpur problems of inclusion were central to the challenge of empowerment and poverty reduction. In Kenya the issue was one of black versus white; in those early years of independence, whites commanded the heights of the economy and the bigger farms, and the challenge was to ensure that opportunity extended equally to black people. In Palanpur the issue was inclusion of the lower castes. And in both settings, gender and physical disability were major barriers to full participation in economic and civic life.

Living and Working with Change and Transition

In the 1980s and 1990s the focus of my work shifted toward the transition economies of China, Eastern and Central Europe, and the former Soviet Union. I had the great pleasure of teaching at People's University in Beijing for the first half of 1988. I learned much from my students—a group with deep experience, in some cases gained during the hard years of the Cultural Revolution. What I discovered firsthand in China, and through my study of the Chinese economic transition, confirmed the importance of removing impediments to the market without destroying existing institutions.

China's economy at the start of their transition in 1979 was highly distorted following a series of calamitous initiatives, notably the Great Leap Forward and the Cultural Revolution. These distortions had left the Chinese people mired in poverty, but they also afforded room for reform—clearly, even mediocre policy would be a distinct improvement in most areas. As a result, the government was able to spur very rapid growth through two major reforms that removed barriers to productive entrepreneurship: the Household Responsibility System in agriculture, and the township and village enterprise movement in the off-farm and urban sectors. These initiatives did much to unleash the great entrepreneurial energies of the Chinese people and increase the market orientation of the economy over the course of a decade. The fact that the reforms were built on the base of existing institutions helped preserve the social cohesion that is crucial to development. For example, China did not privatize or initially even try to restructure the vast state-owned enterprise sector. That decision had obvious costs, but it also prevented a backlash against reform by workers whose jobs would have been threatened.

Another feature of China's drive to reduce poverty—one that impressed me both in the late 1980s and during more recent visits—is the effectiveness of mechanisms for inclusion of the rural poor. On a recent visit (June 2001) to Shanxi Province (a very dry area), for example, I saw terraces that had been constructed on steep hillsides. Such an investment in land can, with the associated water retention, raise agricultural yields dramatically, but it requires real collective action of the sort that government is best suited to coordinate. I also saw collective action in the form of women's microcredit groups, which promoted small entrepreneurship in a way that built assets and capacities. The groups first financed the purchase of a few pigs to be raised by the ablest members. Pigs born to the startup stock were distributed to other members, who also benefited from observing and following the example set by their associates. Eventually, this process generated enough profits to allow the women to invest in other microenterprise activities.

The above examples point to the crucial role of behavior and institutions: these farmers and rural businesspeople not only show strong entrepreneurship but also behave in a way that promotes collective action. Further such behavior both supports institutions and is developed through institutions. Although these rural infrastructure and microcredit mechanisms have not yet reached all parts of the country, China has done far better than most low-income countries in empowering its rural poor to participate economically.

After my time in China, I spent six years focused on the transition economies of Europe and Central Asia as chief economist at the European Bank for Reconstruction and Development (EBRD). This experience reinforced lessons from China and India, in both positive and negative ways.

Investment climate problems and differences were paramount in understanding the transition in Eastern Europe and the former Soviet Union (FSU). Firms there suffered from bureaucratic harassment and both grand and petty corruption, which reduced the rewards to productive entrepreneurship and diverted energies into rent-seeking. Even when the government did succeed in "getting out of the way," its absence was not necessarily constructive. The traumatic experience of much of the FSU confirms that government must act to provide an investment climate for the private sector rather than withdraw and hope that its absence will allow the market to flourish. When the post-Soviet government in the FSU neglected such basic state duties as ensuring security for the citizenry, alternative institutions sprang up. These alternatives, including organized crime, have often discouraged productive investment. The experience of much of Eastern Europe, outside the FSU, while tough, has been much more positive than the FSU itself in large measure because the new and liberated state and polity functioned much better.

The FSU has also provided striking evidence that behaviors, not just institutions and policies, matter in the transition. Both institutions and behaviors were badly corroded by seven decades of Soviet rule. Behaviors that had been adaptive under state socialism, such as smuggling and reliance on connections, now blocked efforts to establish a sound fiscal base and a transparent market economy. In the early years of the transition, behaviors and institutions spiraled downward: old behaviors sabotaged the building of new institutions, and the absence of effective institutions encouraged people to continue relying on old behaviors. The evident surges of both old and new oligarchy in establishing or maintaining positions of wealth and privilege caused profound disillusion in the FSU in the whole process of transitional reform.

Throughout this period, in the 1980s and 1990s, I remained engaged intellectually with India. Although unable to visit as often as I would have liked, I continued to follow the development of Palanpur through my colleagues Jean Drèze, Peter Lanjouw, and Naresh Sharma. I was also interested in the broader transformation of Indian society. And it is no exaggeration to call it a transformation. Over the past decade and more, India has done much to reinvent itself economically, with salutary results for both growth and, apparently, poverty reduction. The Indian experience has shown what a difference improved policies can make. Progress since the beginning of reform in the late 1980s has been greatest in the area of openness: by lowering barriers to competition, India has spurred its private sector to greater productivity. The result has been a decade of rapid growth, far higher than the so-called Hindu rate of growth that prevailed in previous decades. Nevertheless much of Indian reform has been weak and patchy and there are much greater gains to be made. And a great part of Indian society, particularly rural areas, has been left out or has fallen behind.

Palanpur does not appear to have progressed as rapidly as the "average" for India. As a community with two major disadvantages—it is rural, and it is located in Uttar Pradesh, a state that has shown relatively little appetite for reform—Palanpur has seen far fewer of the fruits of growth. Yet even there, on a brief visit to the village in the autumn of 2000, I was impressed to see improvement in a number of casual empirical indicators of poverty reduction. Progress on two of my favorite "eye-ball" indicators, the shoe-to-foot ratio and the ratio of mud houses to brick houses, was undeniable: although it is impossible to be precise, it looked as if both ratios may have risen by 20 or 30 percentage points or more since I first visited Palanpur tin 1974.

In the area of empowerment, particularly empowerment of women, the village seemed to have moved forward as well. Twenty-five or 30 years ago most women, apart from the lowest castes, would never have left the family compound. But now women were developing their own economic activities and were spending more of their time out of the house. Electricity and television had come to the village in the last few years, apparently influencing women's behavior through the images that they brought of women who were active in the workplace and the broader society. There had clearly been a shift in the male-female balance of power. On a later visit (spring 2001) but further east in Uttar Pradesh in Bareilly District, I was amazed to hear a group of village women laugh good-naturedly at an older man as he complained about the changes: when visitors came calling these days, he said, there were often no women at home to make tea. Given the historically humble status of women in the region, their irreverent response would have been inconceivable a quarter-century ago. But our experience of microdata in Palanpur has taught me to be cautious about impressions from quick visits. It is only by painstakingly putting together the microdata sets that one can come to reliable assessments of circumstances and how they change over time.

These transitions continue, and the lessons from them continue to accumulate. In China the constraints imposed by the policy of building on existing institutions have begun to bind more tightly. China has made good use of flexibility and accommodation for two decades, but some of the legacy institutions, for example the banking system and the all-embracing state-owned enterprise, have outlived their usefulness and are fast becoming impediments to further growth. In Russia recent (summer 2001) stories from people trying to run small firms show that the challenge of transition still runs deep. These entrepreneurs complain of daily visits by officials representing the many government offices from which permits are needed. Bureaucratic harassment has become institutionalized—so much so that government officials now work to keep other predators, including organized crime, from encroaching on their lucrative business.

Conclusion: The New Synthesis and Its Fruits

My personal journey has left me with a pragmatic optimism about the possibilities of development that I believe the field of development economics now shares. Since reaching its high-water mark a decade ago, the tide of neoliberalism has ebbed markedly amid the economic disaster in much of the former Soviet Union and the ascendance of China. We now share an understanding that state and market are not substitutes but complements: the state must lay the foundations for the market if the market is to flourish and work its magic. Strong markets and the involvement of poor people in development require a well-functioning state. The closing of this ideological divide about the role of the state has provided a space for sensible development policy.

Beyond this intellectual progress, there are several grounds for optimism:

- We now understand better what good development policy is. A country's development strategy needs to include both policies to improve the investment climate, in order to raise productivity and speed employment and wage growth, and policies to equip and empower poor people to participate in growth.

- We understand that leadership and broad commitment to policies are central to the process of development. It is not enough to design good policies. If they are to be implemented successfully, those policies must have the support of both political leaders and substantial elements of the populace.

- We know more about how international financial institutions such as the World Bank can operate as agents of change. Development strategies need to be comprehensive. Lending should make careful, well-focused, and sparing use of conditionality, which is rarely able to substitute for domestic ownership of a reform. No one agency can do everything—"seeing the whole is not trying to do the whole." Partnership between actors and agencies, based on comparative advantage, is crucial.

Developing countries and donors alike have begun to internalize these lessons, and we are seeing the results of their efforts. Now that excessively prescriptive government planning and tightly closed economies are largely relics of the past, governments are concentrating more on doing what they must do well to spur development. Improvements in macroeconomic stability and openness are being buttressed by improvements in other elements of the investment climate, especially governance. And expansion of educational opportunity, along with the wave of democracy that has swept across the world in the past quarter-century, has led to at least some empowerment of poor people.

For countries that have taken these steps, the result has been more rapid growth and progress on poverty reduction. But we are beginning to see a real separation between developing countries that are making strong progress and those that are not. Countries in this second group—those with weak governance, little empowerment, and feeble integration with the world economy—continue to suffer. Efforts to meet international targets for poverty reduction will hinge on helping these countries do better.

There is much that the rich countries can do to increase the payoffs of reform. First, they can open their markets to external trade, and especially to products from the poorest countries. Recent steps taken by most members of the Organisation for Economic Co-operation and Development (OECD) and reaffirmed at the July 2001 G-8 meeting in Genoa have advanced this agenda substantially. Second, the rich countries can and should increase their aid—the decline over the last two decades, at a time of increasing prosperity in the developed world, is surely morally indefensible. Further, they can target their aid to more effective uses, coordinate their aid programs better, and provide debt relief to countries that will devote the savings to poverty reduction. Finally, they can contribute knowledge and policy help—which, when combined with government ownership of policies, can have even greater effects than financial assistance.

We have, collectively, a great opportunity to make a difference. I believe firmly that when historians look back at the past quarter-century, they will identify as the single most important event the massive—indeed, unprecedented—poverty reduction that has taken place in China. Over the past decade India and many other countries have begun to make major inroads into poverty. But so many are being left out both in those countries that are making strong progress in the aggregate and in those countries which as a whole are showing little growth. With focus and perseverance, we can carry the momentum of poverty reduction which we can now see, right across the developing world.

Fifty Years of Development

Paul Collier, David Dollar, and Nicholas Stern

Annual Meeting of the Latin American and Caribbean Economics
Association, Rio de Janeiro, Brazil, October 2000

Our perspectives on development have changed radically over the past half-century, and indeed over the past decade. New evidence and new theoretical approaches have deepened and shifted the debate. We have a much better understanding of the relationships among markets, governance, and institutions. Our techniques of empirical analysis and the availability of data have advanced dramatically; indeed, one of the encouraging features of the modern analysis of development is its growing respect for evidence. We now have a much less simplistic view of living standards and well-being, and therefore of poverty and inequality. Correspondingly, there is a much stronger analytical focus on understanding the economic and societal processes that enhance education and health—key factors that influence the capabilities, including the spending power, of individuals. In this essay, we provide an interpretative view of the development experiences of the past 50 years, focusing especially on the past 10 years (since much has already been written on the earlier periods).

What was the state of opinion 10 years ago? A 1989 survey of the economics of development provides one summary:

> The ability of governments to plan comprehensively and effectively is now viewed with much greater skepticism than in the years following the Second World War. Thus many would now place equal or greater emphasis on government failure relative to market failure in the balance of the argument than was previously the case with the earlier writers, who concentrated heavily on market failure. The skepticism is

The authors' affiliations are: Paul Collier, Oxford University and World Bank; David Dollar, World Bank; and Nicholas Stern, London School of Economics and World Bank. The views expressed are those of the authors and do not necessarily reflect the official views of the World Bank or its member countries. The authors thank Gerard Caprio, Aart Kraay, and Lyn Squire for valuable contributions. An earlier version of this speech was given at the Annual World Bank Conference on Development Economics in Paris in June 2000. The section "Changes in Development Thinking" is adapted from Stern 1997.

born of experience but one must be careful not to be too sweeping. We have learned much about what governments can do effectively as well as where they are likely to perform badly. Whereas it is possible that they may be damaging to efficiency and growth if they try to exert detailed and universal control of production decisions, governments can be effective with direct action to raise standards of education, health and life expectancy, and in improving infrastructure such as water supply, roads, power. There is much to be learned about how to organize such action but we already know enough to realize that really substantial achievements are possible and to be able to begin to indicate the kinds of policies which will work and those which will not. (Stern 1989: 669)

So, a decade ago those working on development had, by and large, absorbed the lessons of the importance of markets and had moved on to emphasize that in a market economy, public action has the potential to transform the lives of the poor.

What happened in the 1990s? Many, but by no means all, developing and transition economies became more market oriented as a result of price reform, reductions in the size of the public sector, and trade liberalization. Some of these countries, including the largest, achieved spectacular reductions in poverty, but others stagnated, declined, or suffered temporary collapse. On average, the market-oriented reforms worked, but not in a reliable fashion. Our reading of the 1990s is that the reform process too often neglected the institutional foundations necessary if markets are to be effective for poverty reduction. It is not enough to focus attention on "getting prices right"; public action is needed to "get the markets right."

Markets depend on a complex array of public institutions. For example, governments should encourage rather than penalize entrepreneurship and competition, uphold the rule of law, and limit bureaucratic harassment and corruption. In short, they should provide good governance. Services with large externalities or market failures, such as transport, telecommunications, and power infrastructure, require regulation. This role of government as the builder and provider of institutions for the market economy is the theme of *World Development Report 2002: Building Institutions for Markets*.

But providing governance and building institutions to enhance the functioning of markets is only one part of a strategy for promoting development. Markets must work *for the poor*. If poor people are to reap the benefits of market-oriented growth, they need to be able to participate in markets. Thus governments have special responsibilities for ensuring the provision of education and health to poor people. Beyond this, governments can help protect poor people from insecurity; fear of falling into poverty, or deeper into poverty, inhibits people from taking the risks inherent in market participation. Furthermore, poor people need to be empowered to participate politically, so that public action becomes shaped by their priorities. This triad of opportunity, security, and empowerment is the theme of *World Development Report 2000/2001: Attacking Poverty*.

In understanding that triad, it is vital to recognize that opportunity, empowerment, and vulnerability are not simply about raising spending power. More fundamentally, they concern the ability of individuals to shape their own lives in the way they choose. Education, health, and basic democratic rights are crucial to achieving that goal, and not merely as instruments for raising incomes.

The main lessons that we draw from the experiences of the 1990s are that public action in the areas highlighted above is both more important and more difficult than was appreciated at the start of the decade. Effective public action is difficult for economic reasons—it is hard to design effective institutions with the right incentives. (For example, in rich as well as in poor countries, there are intense debates about how to organize schools in order to deliver education.) It is also difficult for social and political reasons: even when we believe we know how to deliver services to the poor, it is often impossible to build a political coalition in support of the change.

The challenges of improving governance and the provision of public services, and their focus on the poor, highlight the importance of institutions, norms, and behaviors for development. If we had to single out one key idea that has risen to prominence in development thinking in the 1990s, that would be it. We cannot call it a new idea; 30 years ago Moses Abramovitz was talking about the "social capacity for development" and how it was determined by history and culture (see Abramovitz and David 1973). The concept has also been well recognized by economic historians such as Schumpeter (see, for example, Schumpeter 1962). A striking expression of this view can be seen in the famous fourteenth-century Siena frescos by Ambrogio Lorenzetti on the "Effects of Good and Bad Government."[1] What we have experienced in

1. Two cities are portrayed. One city's government is counseled by Justice, Wisdom, and Compassion and the other's, by Pride, Wrath, and Avarice. The first city is orderly, happy, and prosperous; the second is poor, corrupt, and oppressed.

the past 10 years, with the growing recognition of the importance of these issues, is a deepening of their theoretical and empirical examination. We will draw attention to a number of examples in what follows.

A particularly powerful example of the importance of norms and behavior and their effect on development is the current spread of the AIDS epidemic. The spread of AIDS can be controlled through relatively simple changes in behavior, especially of high-risk groups such as sex workers and their customers. A few governments, such as those of Senegal and Thailand, have focused on the problem and have carried out successful targeted public campaigns to promote these changes. But in many other places, even where HIV incidence is very high, governments either ignore the problem or fail to target their programs on the high-risk groups. For some countries in Africa, the consequences of this neglect will be catastrophic. Here is a clear case in which the research community can provide real guidance but has so far failed to convince governments of the importance of action.

As thinking about development has changed, so too has what we have come to expect from development agencies such as the World Bank. In the era when much development thinking placed planning at center stage, the Bank helped finance the big projects that were at the heart of many of the plans. When the emphasis shifted to the policy environment, particularly "getting prices right," the Bank promoted stabilization and trade liberalization and financed structural adjustment. Now, the agenda has stronger governance and institutional elements, including helping societies provide effective public services oriented to the poor. This calls for a different role for the Bank—one that puts still more emphasis on learning and knowledge.

In many cases communities have to learn for themselves how to design effective institutions that work in their particular settings. Development agencies can help with some basic principles of design and evaluation, and of course with finance, but appropriate institutions have to be locally tailored for each society. The range of legitimate experiment must therefore be wider for institutional reform than for (say) macroeconomic and trade reform. The Bank, working with its partners, thus needs to combine conviction in those areas of policy where the evidence warrants it with flexibility and a heuristic approach in those areas of institutional design that require experiment.

The next section contains a discussion of experience worldwide from the perspectives we have just described. This leads, in the subsequent section, to a brief summary of the ways in which development thinking has changed. We conclude with an agenda for action and research.

Regional and Country Experiences

Before delving into regional and country experiences, it is important to underline that at a global level, the past several decades have seen great development progress. Table 1 summarizes this progress along various income and nonincome measures. It shows that the developing world as a whole has seen significant income growth, with per capita incomes growing 118 percent over the past 40 years. Equally important, low- and middle-income countries have reduced child mortality rates sharply, have steadily increased life expectancy, and have made great inroads against illiteracy. The numbers given here represent major progress, particularly when judged against the pace of development that prevailed in most parts of the world before the second half of the twentieth century.

Table 1. Indicators of Development Progress

(total change over period)

	GDP (percent), 1960–2000	GDP per capita (percent), 1960–2000	Under-5 mortality rate (per 1,000), 1960–99	Life expectancy at birth (years), 1960–99	Adult illiteracy rate, 15 and over (percentage points), 1970–2000
World	337	118	−112	16	−21
High-income countries	315	200	−31	8	. .
Low- and middle-income countries	456	156	−131	20	−22
East Asia and Pacific	1,207	554	−154	30	−30
Latin America and the Caribbean	362	95	−116	13	−15
Middle East and North Africa	*131*	*16*	−194	21	−35
South Asia	499	148	−140	19	−23
Sub-Saharan Africa	251	19	−95	7	−33

Note: Figures in italics indicate a shorter period than the one specified. For GDP and GDP per capita, period for the Middle East and North Africa is 1974–99. Europe and Central Asia is not included because not enough data are available.

Source: World Bank calculations.

Figure 1. World Poverty, 1820–1998

Number of people living on less than $1 per day (millions)

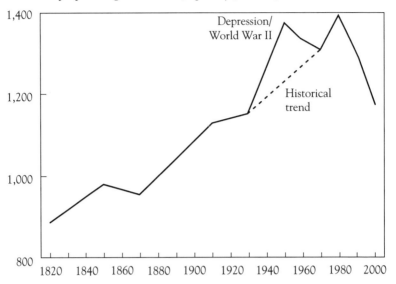

Source: World Bank data and projections.

The last twenty years have been the first fall in total numbers in poverty for two hundred years (see Figure 1). This has been largely due to the very rapid growth over these two decades in China and rising growth rates in India, particularly over the last 7 or 8 years, as both countries have loosened internal restrictions and become more integrated into the world economy. Income per capita in developing countries is now rising faster than in developed countries and given the basis in noting improvements in developing countries this further growth is likely to continue over the next decade (see Figure 2).

And yet it is also clear that individual country and regional experiences with growth and poverty reduction vary enormously. Consider the figures for income poverty, which are available only for a much shorter period than is covered in Table 1. In the 10 years between 1988 and 1997, East Asia's headcount poverty rate (the share of the population living on less than $1 a day) declined by 12 percent per year, while in Eastern Europe and Central Asia the poverty rate increased by nearly 4 percent per year (Figure 3). South Asia has done relatively well on this

Figure 2. World, Industrial, and Developing Country GDP Growth, 1997–2003

Percent change

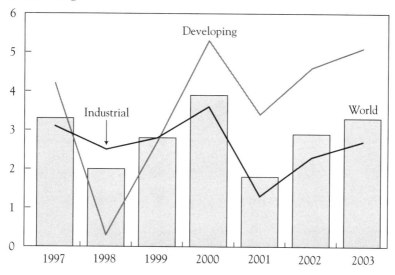

Source: World Bank data and projections.

measure, but poverty reduction in Sub-Saharan Africa, the Middle East and North Africa, and Latin America has been modest at best. (Because these are population-weighted averages of individual country experiences, the East Asian data primarily reflect China's experience and the South Asian data, India's.) One thing that stands out clearly in Figure 3 is that growth and poverty reduction tend to go hand in hand. Their close association reflects the fact that the same historical factors, institutions, and policies that create a good environment for growth also provide a good environment for poor households to move forward (Dollar and Kraay 2001).

But this observation, although of great importance, does not allow us to conclude that growth-enhancing policies alone are sufficient to reduce poverty. First, as we have emphasized, well-being and poverty concern much more than spending power. Second, the process of growth may exclude and dislocate large sections of the population. Hence the need for public action to promote not only growth but also participation and protection.

Figure 3. Growth and Poverty Reduction, by Region, 1988–97
(percent)

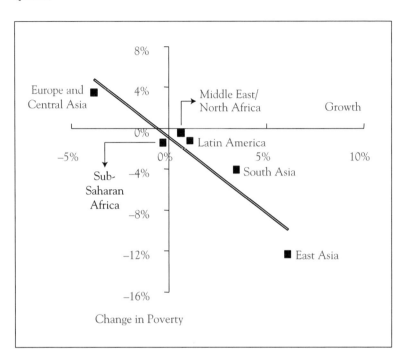

Note: Annual percentage rate of change of the headcount poverty index plotted against annual rate of growth of per capita gross domestic product (GDP); population-weighted average of the countries in each region; $y = -1.4837x - 0.0087$; $R^2 = 0.8883$. The headcount poverty index is the share of the population below a poverty line of $1 (purchasing power parity) per day.
Source: World Bank 2000e.

In this section, we provide our interpretation of some of the important development experiences of recent decades, using examples from every region of the developing world (although of course we cannot cover every country). Our survey reveals that the variation in regional experiences partly reflects the extent of market reform in different countries. But we also want to stress that the impact of market reform depends to a considerable extent on countries' initial conditions, as well as on the development of the complementary institutions that are needed to make markets work well and equitably.

East Asia: China

We begin with China because its extraordinary growth and poverty reduction have been among the most important developments of the past 20 years. In the late 1970s this huge country was emerging from crisis. Its reform began in the 1970s with radical changes in incentives for households and individuals. Most important, for this largely rural society, was the return, over the period 1979–83, of farming to a family basis. Use rights over land, together with some significant price liberalization, transformed individual incentives very rapidly, and agricultural production and household income rose dramatically.

An important aspect of China's reform has been the introduction of new institutions. Indeed, the township and village enterprises (TVEs) were key to China's industrial growth after 1983. (Figure 4 illustrates the

Figure 4. Growth of Township and Village Enterprises (TVEs) in China
(tens of thousands)

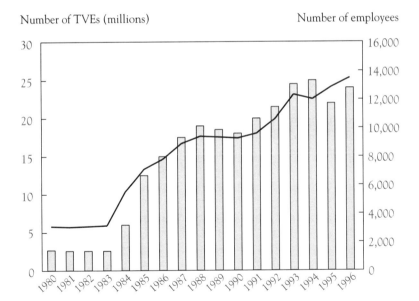

Note: Bars show number of TVEs, line shows number of employees.
Source: State Statistical Bureau, *Chinese Statistical Yearbook*, various years.

rapid growth in TVE employment over this period.) TVEs, although collective, provided incentives that came fairly close to private ownership of small and medium-size factories at a time when overt private property rights would not have been politically acceptable. At the same time China began to open up to foreign trade and to foreign direct investment (FDI). The combination of agricultural reforms, TVEs, greater openness, and, more generally, the encouragement of entrepreneurship and the introduction of market-based incentives yielded remarkable results. After two decades of stagnation, China's economy began to grow rapidly, and the initial benefits accrued to a large extent to the rural population, where poverty was most acute. Between 1978 and 1995, 200 million people were lifted out of absolute poverty in China.

A number of special features help explain why China reaped such spectacular results from strengthened incentives and more open markets. Part of Mao Zedong's economic strategy had been to build self-sufficiency in each province. (Each major province literally produced its own brand of car.) With the many staggering inefficiencies associated with this strategy came large potential gains from interprovincial trade, leading to more specialization and to economies of scale. Provincial self-sufficiency also afforded some protection from the dislocations of change. The large overseas Chinese community played a positive role in China's reform, providing finance, technology, and managerial know-how. Hong Kong entrepreneurs, who did not have a political conflict with Beijing, led the way. Their good results encouraged a later flow of investment from entrepreneurs based in Taiwan, China.[2]

China's advantageous initial conditions also included, notwithstanding the Cultural Revolution of 1966–76, key elements of political stability and social adherence to the rule of law. There was also a fairly sound macroeconomic foundation resulting from the country's high savings rate and cautious macromanagement. Of all the transition economies, China was virtually the only one not beset during its reform period by high inflation. These initial conditions were important because they ensured that the reforms of incentives and prices would yield quick, positive results, thus building broad popular support for reform. Political and macroeconomic stability, together with the size of the country and a highly pragmatic philosophy, also created an environment in which the

---

2. The role of a diaspora has been important for development in other countries too, but its impact, whether positive or negative, depends on the specific historical and political aspects of the separation. See the discussion of the Eastern European and Russian diasporas in "Eastern Europe and Central Asia."

government could afford to experiment with certain reforms before introducing them countrywide.[3]

While China has achieved impressive results so far, it faces important challenges. It is beginning a new stage in which its further growth will depend to a large extent on the emergence of a "true" private sector. The era of TVE-led growth is probably at an end. China's accession to the World Trade Organization (WTO) is a very positive move that will support the market-based approaches, including legal reforms, that are necessary for private sector development. But the country still has a large number of inefficient state enterprises, employing a vast urban work force. These enterprises are supported by a state-dominated financial system that is increasingly beset by nonperforming loans. Following through on market, enterprise, and related financial sector reforms is essential to keeping China on a successful path of growth.

We have focused here on China's growth from the perspective of reform and institutions. It is important to recognize that China entered the reform period with very strong educational and health conditions for a country of its income. For example, life expectancy in 1987 was 68.7 years, and in 1998 it was 69.9 years.

Eastern Europe and Central Asia

It is commonplace to describe China's relatively successful reforms as gradual. Such a description is highly misleading as applied to the dramatic change in its agriculture sector at the end of the 1970s and the early 1980s, which transformed the lives of hundreds of millions. Nevertheless, China's approach and results are often contrasted with the experience of transformation in Eastern Europe and the former Soviet Union (FSU), which underwent what is often described as "shock therapy." In fact, however, there are significant similarities between China and the successful Eastern European reformers (such as Estonia, Hungary, and Poland) and important contrasts between that generally successful group and the deeply problematic reforms in Russia, Ukraine, and other FSU economies.

The Stalinist "overintegration" of the economies of the Soviet bloc meant that the collapse of the Soviet Union was a fundamental

---

3. This pragmatism is reflected in Deng Xiaoping's famous remark, "It does not matter if the cat is black or white as long as it catches mice."

economic shock to all the countries in the region—something that China did not have to face in its early reforms. But countries such as Hungary and Poland were able to reestablish macro stability relatively quickly, rapidly reorienting exports toward the European Union.

The successful Eastern European reformers had several characteristics in common with China. Long-term commitment to reform across a very broad section of society was deep and was never in serious doubt. The importance of building institutions was well understood, although different approaches were followed in different countries. In Eastern Europe, as in China, there was a living memory of a market system, and the four decades under Stalinism had not completely eroded fundamental social adherence to the rule of law. There too, constructive diasporas contributed capital and knowledge. Thus, in these Eastern European economies, stable political commitment to reform, macro stabilization, attention to institution-building, stronger private incentives, and trade openness yielded good results fairly quickly.

Russia and other FSU countries unfortunately had much less favorable initial conditions than the Eastern European countries. Here, the Communist Party was more deeply established, and there was a real fear in the early 1990s that it might return to power. On the one hand, this encouraged reformers to move very quickly with a (seriously flawed) mass privatization; on the other hand, it was harder to attract investment and make reforms succeed. The problem of a rigid, interlocked economic structure was still deeper than in Central and Eastern Europe. The Russian diaspora in the United States and Western Europe mostly dated to many decades previously and was not closely connected with the homeland. Far from experiencing net inflows, Russia suffered massive capital flight over the decade. The longer period of communist rule in Russia compared with Eastern Europe meant that adherence to the rule of law was weak. Furthermore, Russia had the kinds of natural resources that, when combined with a *nomenklatura* tradition of state capture by a closed elite, were highly susceptible to appropriation by oligarchs.

The outcome of all these influences was that in the Russian context it was harder to get good results from reform and thus harder to build, support, and sustain reforms. Indeed, the early experiences of the market economy for most Russians were marked by the ravages of hyperinflation and the spectacle of asset-grabbing on an enormous scale. The result has been a fundamental crisis of confidence in reform that is itself an obstacle to moving forward.

Russia is now enjoying a period of political stability and emerging growth that offers an opportunity for a new start. Taking that opportunity will require careful attention to the investment climate and institutional reform and will involve, in many cases, confronting the vested interests that established themselves all too firmly in the earlier period of reform.

South Asia: India

Turning to South Asia, India's experience over five decades is basically a microcosm of the changes in development thinking. Although the formal planning system instituted in the early 1950s had been largely discredited by the mid-1960s, for the three decades following independence India had an economic system dominated by government protection and regulation and closed, to a large extent, to the global economy. When combined with India's record of stable macroeconomic policies, this system produced a fairly consistent but unspectacular outcome: growth of gross domestic product (GDP) that averaged 3.5 percent per year. With population growth at 2.2 percent per year, per capita income rose slowly, and there was little discernible reduction in the high level of poverty. This pace of change could be seen at the micro level as well; for example, in 1980 India was producing cars that looked about the same as cars in 1950.

Over the past two decades India has opened up to the world economy. The loosening of macroeconomic controls in the second half of the 1980s generated a macro crisis in 1991 that led to aggregate retrenchment but also to an acceleration of reforms. India has reduced its external barriers to both foreign trade and foreign investment and has begun to dismantle many of the other regulations and restrictions on investment and production. An important point in discussing India is that many of the restrictions are at the state level, and hence the pattern of liberalization has varied across the country.

Since 1993, aggregate growth in India has been remarkably rapid, averaging about 7 percent per year. The experience of the past six to seven years suggests that India may have now embarked on an extended period of rapid growth. Over these years its growth has been comparable with or faster than that of China and much faster than in the countries of the Organisation for Economic Co-operation and Development (OECD).

India is unique among developing countries in having 50 years of household distribution data of reasonable quality. In a series of papers based on these surveys, Ravallion and Datt have estimated that the poverty rate decreases 1 percent for every 1 percent increase in net domestic product per capita, and their decomposition of changes in poverty based on Indian data found that 87 percent of the observed decline in poverty was accounted for by the growth component rather than by changes in distribution (Datt and Ravallion 1998a, 1998b; Ravallion and Datt 1999).

Thus, reform has delivered growth in India, and growth has delivered poverty reduction. However, reform and growth have been uneven across states. In the postreform period, poverty has been declining in the states of Andhra Pradesh, Gujarat, Karnataka, Kerala, Maharashtra, Punjab, and West Bengal but not in Bihar, Madhya Pradesh, Orissa, Rajasthan, and Uttar Pradesh. The states in the first group have better human capital and social indicators and, except for Punjab, are coastal (Srinivasan 2000). For both reasons they are better placed to benefit from economic reforms.

One of our important projects in the Research Group of the World Bank is investigation, through enterprise surveys, of the regulatory and investment climate at the state level in India. Preliminary indications are that, in general, the first group of states, in which poverty has been declining, has less burdensome and distortionary regulatory regimes than the second group. Better governance—in particular, delivery of services plus efficient regulation and good location—is combining with openness to produce growth and poverty reduction in some states. Others lag behind.

As we have emphasized throughout, increases in well-being imply much more than rising incomes. Still more striking, and arguably of still greater importance, have been the changes in health and education in many parts of India. In Kerala life expectancy is now greater than in China, and in Andhra Pradesh and Himachal Pradesh education systems have been transformed (see Drèze and Sen forthcoming).

Again, from this experience we see the importance of both good macro-level policies—stability and openness—and effective governance and service delivery at the more micro level, particularly in the promotion of health and education.

Latin America and the Caribbean

Latin America's experience has interesting parallels with India's. In the 1960s and 1970s Latin American economic strategy, influenced by the thinking of export pessimists such as Raúl Prebisch, focused on import substitution. At the same time the continent relied much more on imported capital than did India. The combination of import protection and external borrowing eventually gave rise to macroeconomic instability—unsustainable fiscal deficits and external debt, high inflation, and volatile exchange rates. Thus, the key reform for the region has been macroeconomic stabilization combined with greater openness to trade. The average inflation rate of Latin American economies declined 54 percentage points between the 1986–90 period and the 1991–93 period.

As with India, Latin America's macro-level reforms have been both heartening and disappointing. On the positive side, the increase in Latin American growth rates is what might be predicted from cross-country growth analysis: 2 percentage points higher growth over the medium term (Easterly, Loayza, and Montiel 1997). On the negative side, the growth benefits were reduced by the slower growth of OECD economies in the 1990s, which had a large spillover effect on the developing world. Furthermore, with the East Asian "miracle" performance as a reference, many in the region (and elsewhere) may have expected a lot more from the reforms. Paul Krugman used the Latin American experience to assert that "the real economic performance of countries that had recently adopted Washington consensus policies . . . was distinctly disappointing" (Krugman 1995: 41).

The problem here was that development economists attributed too much of East Asia's success to macro stability and openness. These are, admittedly, important ingredients, but they need to be complemented by institutional development, notably improvements in the delivery of public services and in public sector efficiency—as indeed happened in East Asia. Furthermore, Latin America's progress in growth and poverty reduction was hampered by its extremely unequal distribution of assets, both land and human capital. These are problems that can be addressed through effective government institutions and policies. With macro reforms largely accomplished, the importance of these other issues appears all the more critical.

Middle East and North Africa

The Middle East and North Africa suffered the paradox of high investment in human and physical capital juxtaposed with stagnation. GDP per capita declined at a rate of 0.8 percent a year in the 1980s and increased only 1.1 percent a year in the 1990s. And yet rates of investment in the Arab world have been impressively high, averaging more than 28 percent of GDP in 1974–85 and more than 22 percent in 1986–97. Although these are lower than the very high rates achieved in East Asia, they are several percentage points higher than in other developing regions (Makdisi, Fattah, and Limam 2000). Similarly, the region has seen impressive growth in the educational attainment of its population. The gross enrollment rate at the secondary level increased from 42 percent in 1980 to 64 percent in 1996. These are close to the rates for East Asia, and better than those for other regions (World Bank 1999a).

Given these statistics, the central question facing any student of development in the Middle East and North Africa must be, why have such high rates of investment in physical and human capital generated so little additional output? Although the detailed answers will be country-specific, two general causes stand out. First, physical investment has not been directed to the most productive activities, in large part because it has been managed by the public sector and often dominated by political rather than market influences. Second, the institutional structure of the labor market has systematically misallocated labor, especially educated labor, for essentially the same reason. Consider each in turn.

The simplest measure of the size of the state in economic activity is the ratio of public expenditure to GDP. In 1977 this ratio stood at 38 percent in the Middle East and North Africa; by 1997 it was a still sizable 28 percent. By way of comparison, the share in Latin America in 1977 was 19 percent, and in East Asia it was 12 percent (Salehi-Isfahani 2000). The oil price increases of the 1970s allowed both the oil exporters and the recipients of assistance from the oil-exporting countries to finance a strategy of development that was dominated by the public sector. Employment in the public sector was both large and well rewarded. In the early 1990s the central government wage bill amounted to almost 10 percent of GDP in the region. That share was less than 5 percent in every other region except Sub-Saharan Africa, where it was 6.7 percent (Pissarides 2000).

Investment in the public sector was rarely subject to a market test, and the quality of investment was very weak. Furthermore, policies were adopted to protect and nurture the growing public sector to the detriment of private investment and entrepreneurship. Consequently, net private transfers in several countries were negative, despite the inflow of worker remittances, as capital was moved abroad. In Egypt, for example, the stock of savings held abroad is estimated to have been $83 billion in 1991, or 271 percent of GDP (Diwan and Squire 1995). This combination of unproductive public investment and private capital flight goes a long way toward explaining the disappointing growth performance.

Turning to human capital, the institutional structure of the labor market was such that for many individuals, rent-seeking yielded a higher return than more productive and growth-enhancing activities. Two elements of the labor market in the Middle East and North Africa were especially important. First, high government wages attracted the most qualified personnel to the public sector. Second, market flexibility was limited by a variety of measures designed to protect existing employment, with the end result that economies were slow to adjust to changing circumstances.

The need to achieve a more productive environment for entrepreneurship, greater efficiency in the public sector, and more complementarity between the public and private sectors is the main lesson to be drawn from the region's experience. Some progress has been made; for example, the fall in the price of oil has forced many countries to shrink their public sectors. A good climate for private investment has yet to be established, however. Major macroeconomic imbalances have been reduced in most countries, but structural reforms are proceeding slowly, at best. One revealing statistic is that since the mid-1990s the region has seen the smallest growth in FDI of any region in the world, and today its share of total FDI flows to developing countries is only 2.5 percent (Nabli 2000).

Sub-Saharan Africa

Sub-Saharan Africa has been experiencing economic and social catastrophe. On average, per capita GDP is lower now than in 1980, although during the 1990s performance became more divergent, with rapid growth in a few countries juxtaposed against rapid decline elsewhere. Socially, life expectancy is now starting to decline, and the incidence of civil conflict is high and rising. The economic catastrophe was associated with a capital-hostile environment and poor public service delivery.

The region has suffered massive capital flight: by 1990 around 40 percent of Africa's private wealth was held outside the continent, a higher share than in any other region (Collier, Hoeffler, and Pattillo 2001). As a result, Africa had far less private capital per member of the labor force than other regions. Despite this scarcity of capital, evidence suggests that the return on investment has been around one-third lower in Africa than in other regions (Collier and Gunning 1999, for the period 1965–89). Evidently, Africans moved their wealth out of Africa at least in part because returns, taking account of risk, were unattractive. Africa, with the worst investor risk ratings of any region, has been perceived, both by Africans themselves and by foreign investors, as a capital-hostile environment.

Low private investment was offset by high public investment, much of it financed by aid; Africa has the highest ratio of public to private capital of any region. High public investment, however, did not produce good public service delivery. On many indicators—education, health, infrastructure—Africa compares unfavorably with other regions.

Several factors have conspired to produce the capital-hostile environment. An economic geography argument (e.g., Bloom and Sachs 1998) is that a combination of malaria, poor soils, and the remoteness of much of the population from the coast intrinsically disadvantages the continent. Yet despite these serious drawbacks, Africa grew reasonably rapidly until the mid-1960s, and some landlocked, malaria-ridden parts of the continent did well during the 1990s. The World Bank has primarily focused on weak institutions and poor policy as the problem. In the Country Policy and Institutional Assessment, through which World Bank staff annually rate policy in over 100 countries, Africa has consistently had the worst ratings. Overvalued exchange rates and high taxation of exports have been typical policies in Africa, although during the 1990s there was significant improvement. A final explanation is that private investment has been discouraged by poor public service delivery, in particular in telecommunications, electric power supply, and transport. As macroeconomic policies improve, poor service delivery and weak governance and institutions increasingly appear to be the binding constraints.

Why are public service delivery and governance so problematic? On a general level, governments appear to have been less concerned with using the public sector for service delivery than with extending patronage through jobs. For example, a study of Ghana found that in the public sector, wages were 25 percent higher if the worker was from the locally dominant tribe (Collier and Garg 1999). Expenditures on inputs such as textbooks and drugs are only half as large in relation to the wage bill in Africa as in South Asia.

As long as the public sector delivered jobs, it was not subject to close scrutiny. For example, a survey in Uganda in 1991 found that only 2 percent of the money released by the Ministry of Finance for primary schools actually reached the schools (Reinikka 2001). In the extreme, public employees not only failed to deliver the services they were supposed to provide but were actively harmful. In Côte d'Ivoire the private sector went on strike against police extortion; the outcome was that business was easier to conduct with the police confined to barracks than when they were on the streets.

Yet the experience of the 1990s shows that Africa's economic catastrophe can be reversed. Uganda provides a hopeful example. Once the government reformed macroeconomic and trade policies, the country was able to attract back Ugandan capital; about 17 percent of private wealth was repatriated during 1993–97 (Collier, Hoeffler, and Pattillo 2001). Empowering the rural population has helped public services improve. For instance, Uganda's Ministry of Finance began alerting local communities each time it released money for schools by sending them information posters; by 1999, 90 percent of the money was getting through. This increased transparency of the budget is an instructive example of how an institutional change can lead to better services.

The social catastrophe of falling life expectancy is largely attributable to the rapid spread of AIDS. Again, this is amenable to policy. The spread of AIDS reflects a failure of public services to focus effectively on the problem. The epidemic can be radically slowed if prostitutes are persuaded to use condoms and undergo health checks—behavioral changes that have been demonstrated to be well within the capability of public health campaigns (World Bank 1997a). African countries such as Uganda are moving on this issue, but some countries remain locked in denial.

The social catastrophe of civil conflict has roots in economic failure. The incidence of conflict in Africa is explicable in terms of five features of its economy, as outlined in Collier and Hoeffler 2000: (a) high dependence on primary commodity exports offers opportunities for rebel organizations to finance themselves through predation; (b) large disaffected diasporas provide a further source of rebel finance; (c) low income weakens the ability of the government to finance defense; (d) slow growth provides insufficient attractive employment opportunities for uneducated youths; and (e) geographic dispersion of the population makes it harder for the government to control its territory. The capital-hostile environment proved conducive to civil conflict. Rapid growth and the consequent economic diversification, job creation, and urbanization can make African societies radically safer.

International Developments

Aside from these individual country and regional experiences, there have been important developments in the international arena that inevitably influence development strategy. The biggest change has been the emergence of private capital flows from rich to poor countries. Economic models have always suggested that private capital should flow from locations in which capital is abundant to locations in which it is scarce. Throughout the 1960s and 1970s, however, such flows remained modest on any scale. In our view, these flows were constrained both by weaknesses in international capital markets and, as noted above, by poor domestic policies and institutions that discouraged business and entrepreneurship in many developing countries. During the past 20 years, and especially during the past 10, there has been a tremendous surge in private capital flows to the developing world, the result of more efficient capital market institutions and policy reform in many developing countries.

These capital flows carry a potential for strong externalities, both positive and negative. On the positive side, direct investment, in particular, can be an important vehicle for bringing new technology and management skills to the developing world. On the negative side, the potential adverse spillover from capital flows was made amply evident by the recent financial crisis in East Asia. No doubt, macroeconomic policy mistakes were made. What is new for the developing world is the way in which apparently modest policy errors were amplified by capital market reactions into crises of truly large proportions. The East Asian financial crisis was an experience that highlighted a key theme of this paper: the importance of complementing macroeconomic, trade, and capital account reform with institutional development—in this case, development of institutions for monitoring, regulating, and supervising banks, other financial institutions, and credit markets.

A fundamental international development of the past 10 years has been the end of the Cold War and the rise of democratic political institutions worldwide. Virtually every region of the developing world has seen major democratic revolutions. In the early 1990s it was hoped that political liberalization would lead to economic reform and better public services. The experience of the 1990s showed, however, that we must be wary of asserting the existence of a tight and inexorable link between political reform and economic reform. Some of the best performers in terms of economic reform and actual reduction of poverty (China and Vietnam) were not noted for formal democratic institutions, while some of the prominent democratizers (Nicaragua and Russia, for example) remain plagued with poor economic policies. On the positive side, no famine has ever occurred in a democratic country with a free press and regular elections (see Drèze and Sen 1995). Political freedoms and democratic institutions provide for protection and participation. Recent studies on the longer-term relationship between political structure and economic performance suggest that democracy is of particular importance in ethnically diverse societies (Collier 2000; Elbadawi and Sambanis forthcoming; Reynal-Querol forthcoming). Unfortunately, the region with the greatest ethnic diversity, Africa, has to date had the least democratic politics.

Finally, there has been a revolution in information technology, international communications, and global transport. Ideas spread much faster today because of innovations such as the Internet. The changes in transport and communications have spawned global production that was simply not imaginable 40 years ago. Trade in goods has changed because different components of a particular product can easily be produced in different locations around the world in a coordinated fashion. These changes have arguably had an even greater effect on trade in services. It is much easier to conduct international trade in financial services or consulting services than just a decade ago. Software companies in California can forward computer programs to firms in Bangalore to be worked on during India's daylight hours and then get them back for the next California workday. The technological developments provide an unprecedented opportunity for developing countries to integrate with the global economy.

Drawing Lessons from Experience

From the regional experiences and international developments of the 1990s, we take the following key lessons:

1. Growth can spur poverty reduction.

2. Macro stability, open trade regimes, and a vibrant private sector facilitate growth.

3. Good governance and good policies have a crucial role in these processes. Governments should provide or foster the institutions that make markets work efficiently, thereby promoting entrepreneurship,

competition, and a positive investment climate. Weak institutions, poor governance, and unsound policies can cause market reforms to go badly awry, with great costs, particularly for the poor.

4. Combating poverty involves much more than fostering sound market-oriented growth. It involves:

- Enhancing the capabilities, particularly in education and health, that are fundamental to well-being and that, moreover, make possible participation in market opportunities

- Promoting people's empowerment—their influence over their political, social, and economic environment—which is of basic direct importance to well-being and defending participation

- Providing protection against economic, political, social, and natural vulnerabilities, including those arising from market reforms.

We will comment briefly on some aspects of these lessons.

Macroeconomic and Trade Policy

We do not need to go into great detail on macroeconomic and trade policy because the relevant lessons have, on the whole, already been drawn by developing country policymakers. Easterly (2000) looks at a wide range of macro policy indicators, such as the inflation level, the black-market premium, and financial depth, and shows not only that the average quality of policy has improved in the developing world but also that the dispersion of policies has declined enormously. For example, the median inflation rate of developing countries was cut in half between 1982 and 1997, from about 15 to 7 percent. More important, at the end of the 1990s only 5 percent of all developing countries had inflation above 10 percent. There has been an even more dramatic decline in the black-market premium, which is an indicator of macroeconomic instability as well as of the restrictiveness of the trade regime. The 95 percent confidence interval on the black-market premium stretched from 10 to 40 percent in the mid-1980s but had declined to a range of 2–8 percent by the end of the 1990s. In practice, this means that today there are more developing countries in which firms operate in a stable price environment and can easily purchase foreign exchange to participate in the global economy.

Institutions

With the macro battle increasingly won, attention has shifted to the importance of institutions and governance for creating a good investment climate. Our discussion above emphasized that although large numbers of developing countries have undertaken macro reforms, the investment and growth responses have varied considerably. The different responses result to a large extent from differences in the functioning of taxation, regulation, the rule of law, and infrastructure, and these differences, in turn, can be traced to public institutions and behavior. There is no single magic bullet for increasing private investment following macro reform. Survey evidence suggests that different problems constrain investment in different countries and in the same country at different times. An effective government builds a mechanism for continuous feedback from domestic investors to keep track of changing problems. This is one reason why it is not sensible to focus on potential foreign investors while hoping that local investors are captive. Both the government and potential foreign investors get, or at least should get, their information about investment conditions to a large extent from local investors. Generally, what is good for domestic investment is also good for foreign investors.

Investors seek a stable institutional environment that is governed by the rule of law, not by arbitrary bureaucratic decisionmaking. All too often, bureaucratic harassment cripples entrepreneurship and the effectiveness of investment. In such circumstances promises of discretionary sweetheart deals negotiated between a foreign investor and a minister of trade or finance are not the answer. A firm offered an attractive deal might reasonably fear that a future entrant might secure even more favorable terms and so drive it out of business. Before the firm will invest, it must be compensated for such risks by up-front benefits that are costly to the society and perhaps also to the government. Essential to the stability and predictability of government is equal treatment. Governments often try to reassure investors, but sometimes their attempts actually make the problem worse.

Here is Mikhail Gorbachev in 1990, when he was president of the Soviet Union, trying to persuade foreign investors to commit themselves:

> Those [companies] who are with us now have good prospects of participating in our great country . . . [whereas those who wait] will remain observers for years to come—*we will see to it*. (*International Herald Tribune*, 5 June 1990; italics added)

Gorbachev clearly saw the problem that firms, faced with high uncertainty, would simply delay in making irreversible commitments. His intervention, however, probably made things worse. By threatening unspecified arbitrary action against future investors, he was confirming the worst fears of his audience.

A second argument for equal treatment in a stable and predictable environment is that otherwise governments may disadvantage domestic investors. In high-risk environments, foreign investors have various strategies for risk reduction: they can get political risk insurance, and they can use diplomatic channels to gain some protection. This is one reason why foreign investors build international consortia, so that in the event of trouble many foreign governments and large banks have an interest in pressuring the host government. Domestic investors often lack this protection. They either seek foreign partners or simply move their assets out of the country. The solution is not to create high but equal payoffs to political maneuvering for business purposes but to reduce those payoffs for both domestic and foreign investors.

Governments with poor risk ratings often try to commit themselves to rule-based behavior through national investment codes. Those perceived as the most risky—notably, African and Eastern European governments—may benefit from the additional credibility of signing an international code. Indeed, since actions by one government probably affect how investors perceive risks in neighboring countries, the resulting externality may justify some attempt at coordinating international discipline. However, the attempt two years ago to draw up such a code was abandoned because of opposition from some developing country governments. A further reason for internationally (or at least regionally) coordinated action is to prevent a "race to the bottom" in deals for investors. This is particularly important within South-South trade blocs. The combination of high external barriers and internal free trade places governments at a disadvantage vis-à-vis investors. A foreign investor can bargain among governments in the bloc, locating in the country that offers most while marketing within the whole bloc and benefiting from protectionist rents.

Many of the risks that investors face, however, come not from the high politics of government policy but from the workings of the government bureaucracy. If the commercial courts are corrupt, investors will build in a margin for the uncertainty of contract enforcement. If tax collectors are corrupt, investors will build in a margin for the uncertainty of tax demands. If customs officers arbitrarily delay shipments of inputs, firms will carry large inventories, building in a margin for the cost of financing them. All these margins choke off and distort investment. There is very clear cross-country evidence that the rule of law and the related issues of bureaucratic harassment, criminality, and corruption have a large effect on both domestic and foreign private investment.

Delivery of Public Services

As we have argued, weak governance and institutions act as a tax on investors, implying a higher expected return to justify an investment and resulting in less investment than would otherwise occur. Poor public service delivery has a similar effect. Some services—transport infrastructure and the public power grid, for example—directly affect firms and investors. Surveys of firms often reveal that these are key bottlenecks. The unreliability of the power supply in many developing countries means that any significant investment requires its own power production; this can double the costs of power to the firm, in comparison with the amount it would pay if it could buy reliable power from an efficiently regulated and managed power sector.

Other public services, notably health and education, have direct benefits for individuals and indirect benefits for the investment climate. An educated and healthy work force—that is, strong human capital—can make a big difference to reliability and effective operations, thereby complementing physical investment.

Providing effective public services requires resources. There is growing evidence, however, that in many cases lack of resources is not the key problem for service delivery. We cannot review this evidence in detail here, but Table 2 suggests that weak reform may also be associated with wasteful expenditure and poor delivery.

The table highlights five developing countries that are noted reformers. Government consumption in these countries has, on average, been relatively low (8.8 percent of GDP in 1990) and was virtually unchanged in the 1990s (9.5 percent of GDP in 1998). Also included are some developing countries that have not done so well with reform. These (the "others" in the table) tended to have higher government consumption at the beginning of the 1990s (18.7 percent of GDP), and this share rose over the decade to 21.3 percent by 1998.

Table 2. Government Consumption, Selected Developing Countries, 1990 and 1998

(percentage of GDP)

Country	1990	1998
Reformers		
Ghana	9.3	10.3
India	11.4	10.5
Mexico	8.4	9.4
Uganda	7.5	9.6
Vietnam	7.5	7.6
Average	8.8	9.5
Others		
Angola	34.5	34.7
Burkino Faso	14.9	14.7
Congo, Rep.	13.8	14.3
Jamaica	14.0	21.6
Kenya	18.7	16.1
Ukraine	16.5	26.1
Average	18.7	21.3

Note: Government consumption includes military spending, administration, and subsidies, as well as spending on education and health.

Source: World Bank data.

Although the reformers recorded about half the level of recurrent government spending as the "others" (which are much less committed to reform), they did much better in the 1990s in actually providing critical social services. In the reform group, infant mortality declined from 74.3 per 1,000 live births in 1990 to 64.8 in 1998, and the secondary school enrollment rate increased from 55.1 to 59.9 percent over the same period. Among the slow reformers, the infant mortality rate increased between 1990 and 1998 from 46.0 to 54.2, and the secondary school enrollment rate declined from 54.2 to 47.4 percent.[4]

---

4. The reader may wonder why the *level* of infant mortality is so high for the reformers. The reason is that we deliberately included some of the poorest countries that became noted reformers in the 1990s. For the reform group, (population-weighted) average per capita GDP was $1,732 in 1990, less than half the $3,930 average for the slower reformers. Although the reform countries were spending much less per person on total government services, they were achieving significant progress.

The point is that many countries spend a lot of money on public services but achieve little in the way of results. Too often, the public sector has been used as a means of patronage for the well-connected, through employment generation, rather than as an instrument for delivery of services to the larger community and to the poor. But even when the government wants to use public expenditure for the benefit of the poor, it is difficult to devise institutions that achieve this objective. If norms of social responsibility are weak among public employees, strong incentives or sanctions may be needed in order to change behavior. Further evidence that political leadership and public action can have powerful effects is accumulating (see World Bank 2000e). Examples from India include the positive influence of Bangalore's public "scorecards" for organizations on local services and the expansion of enrollment and educational services in Andhra Pradesh and Himachal Pradesh.

The lesson we draw from experience is that the efficiency of public service delivery is at least as important as the volume of resources devoted to the services. The example of school funds in Uganda, cited above, is a case in point: it hardly matters how much money from the budget is allocated to primary education if only 2 percent of the funds actually reaches schools. The simple change of publicizing the amount of money that should reach each school had a huge effect on behavior and on the educational services ultimately delivered to the community.

Financial Sector

The importance of the financial sector emerges in several ways from our survey of experiences. First, some countries (for example, in the Middle East and North Africa) have had high investment and little growth, indicating that investment efficiency has been poor. Recent research has established that the financial sector plays a significant role, not in directly raising the quantity of investment, but rather in improving its quality. That is, there is no significant link between financial reform and savings, but there is substantial evidence (from firm, industry, and cross-country data) that better and deeper financial systems spur growth through a better allocation of savings. Recent studies show, for example, that countries with deeper financial systems did a better job of taking credit away from loss-making firms and reallocating it to profitable investments.

A second key experience of recent years bearing on the financial system was the East Asian crisis. Weak supervision and regulation of the financial system not only lead to misallocation in good times but can contribute to genuine crisis when external shocks hit.

When it works well, finance contributes importantly to the efficiency of investment and to growth. When it malfunctions, as has been demonstrated in many recent crises around the world, it lowers both, as well as the quantity of investment as banks retreat—usually for some time thereafter. What can developing countries do to make finance work well?

Finance is different from other sectors in its distinctive combination of information asymmetries (providers of funds know less about the ultimate employment of the monies than do users) and intertemporal trade (a euro today in exchange for the promise of a euro, plus some return, tomorrow). Given this information problem, which affects both insiders and outsiders, robust financial systems—systems that can support growth and do not lead to crisis—are those in which, as *World Development Report 1998* put it, there are many "watchful eyes" overseeing the intermediaries.

There are three possible monitors: owners, markets, and supervisors. Authorities can do more to strengthen each. Owners will have the incentive to obtain and act on information if they have something at stake—their current capital in the bank, future profits, or potential liability should they fail. By contrast, when bankers can borrow their capital, so that they can default on the loans and lose nothing, and can transfer their losses easily to the government, we should not expect significant monitoring by owners.

The market, in the form of creditors, can act as a monitor as well. If creditors believe that they will lose their investment if a bank fails, and if they have reliable and prompt information, research shows that they will discipline banks, pulling out as risk-taking rises. Forcing banks to issue uninsured junior debt at regular intervals is a promising way to encourage this monitoring.

Finally, supervisors need reinforcement. If they are paid in line with most civil service scales, they will lag their private sector counterparts substantially—a proven recipe for, at best, weak skills and, at worst, corruption. Many industrial countries pay supervisors and central bankers above government scale. Tying regulators' hands—requiring certain interventions as banks' real net worth declines—may also be an idea whose time has come.

With all these monitors working together, banking stands a chance of functioning well. Robust intermediation also requires diversification, but most developing countries are too small for this to be possible within their borders. Sixty countries have financial systems that, in total, are equal to or smaller than the balance sheet of some credit unions, and two countries out of three, with a total population of 800 million, have financial systems whose assets are less than $10 billion (World Bank 1998). Even if the banks diversify inside such small systems, they will still go bust regularly. The key is broader diversification through regional banking systems and openness to good foreign banks (as in southern Africa, Argentina, and Mexico).

The international community has a role to play here. The World Bank and the International Monetary Fund (IMF) have developed a joint Financial Sector Assessment Program to highlight key vulnerabilities and developmental issues in financial systems. They are also participating in a variety of fora to assist in the development of international standards in accounting, auditing, bank supervision, capital markets regulation, corporate governance, and other dimensions. Applying these standards in different contexts requires a sensitive rather than a formulaic approach. Much remains to be done to rein in bouts of excessive risk-taking and to rewrite regulations for intermediaries in such a way as to dampen booms and busts in international capital flows. While developing countries can encourage this move, upgrading their own regulatory environments will be essential for mitigating crises and stimulating growth.

Changes in Development Thinking

We have put most of the weight in this essay on development experiences and on the lessons from them. This emphasis reflects our judgment that changes in thinking on development have arisen primarily from experience. Here, we want to provide a sketch of how development thinking has changed over the decades, in response not only to the experiences we highlighted above but also to developments in economics. Indeed, our emphasis and language in describing change have been strongly micro and structural. One reason is the changes that have occurred in perceptions of the meaning of poverty. Another is the increasing focus of the profession both on the way in which markets and organizations function in an imperfect world and on how change comes about. To some extent, this shift has reflected developments in other social sciences.

Many economists in the 1950s and 1960s argued, from a number of perspectives, that markets and incentives worked inadequately in developing countries and that governments should therefore play a major role in determining the allocation of resources, and particularly of investment. In this, the economists of the 1950s were reacting to the experiences of colonialism and the Great Depression, which suggested that capitalism and external markets would not promote broad-based development of the economy and society in poor countries. They were also influenced by the achievements of the Soviet Union—a perspective that was to change over time—and by the experience of wartime planning in the United Kingdom. Economists differed over strategies for government direction—for example, in the debates on balanced versus unbalanced growth—but the desirability of government intervention in the economies of developing countries commanded broad agreement. Nevertheless, there were dissents from this apparent consensus—in development economics, for example, by Peter Bauer and Gottfried Haberler, and against planning by political philosophers such as Friedrich von Hayek (see, for example, Bauer 1972; Haberler and Koo 1985: Hayek 1984).

Many economists from both industrial and developing countries were studying the techniques of planning and advising on them. The predilection for planning and direct controls in the profession was in many cases accompanied by pessimism concerning the prospects for exports from developing countries—a pessimism associated particularly with Hans Singer (1950) and Raúl Prebisch (1950). Thus, import-substitution industrialization was recommended by many, even though the issues concerning planning and import substitution were logically distinct.

A central viewpoint on the macroeconomics of development was formalized in the two-gap model, in which Hollis Chenery played a leading role (see Bruno and Chenery 1962). The two gaps were between saving and investment and in the balance of trade. Export pessimism was embodied in a perceived constraint on exports; domestic inflexibilities were manifested in fixed import requirements for investment. Foreign aid, seen through the optic of these models, could be particularly productive in allowing investment to expand by overcoming the constraint on its foreign-exchange component. In both the planning model and the two-gap model, prices played a minimal role, and production techniques offered little choice, with fixed coefficients being a fairly universal assumption.

The 1950s and 1960s brought intense work on aggregate models of economic growth for both industrial and developing countries. Those for industrial countries were predominantly for only one sector, but those for developing countries gave dualism a prominent role. Particularly influential was Lewis's (1954) model of economic growth with unlimited supplies of labor. In it, the process of development was depicted as a transfer of resources out of a traditional sector into an advanced sector, with the growth of the advanced sector being driven by the investment of profits generated in that sector. Taking these various strands together, economic debate in the 1950s and 1960s can be seen as being focused on growth through industrialization and import substitution, with the government playing a central role in the process.

The late 1960s and 1970s brought greater emphasis on the application of basic microeconomic principles. Concern about dubious industrial and project decisions taken in the face of distorted domestic prices, or without any reference to prices, led many economists to work on the measurement of price distortion and on assessment of the consequences of some of the industrial and trade policies that had been followed during the previous decades. Many studies emerged on such topics as effective protection, domestic resource cost, and shadow prices. In economic theory, academics were becoming much more concerned than previously about problems of economic information and incentives and the way in which contractual arrangements developed to take into account or alleviate some of these problems. From this perspective there was particularly intense study during the 1970s and into the 1980s of rural factor markets and institutions, especially with regard to labor, land, and credit. To be sure, in this theoretical research the perspective on "institutions" was a fairly narrow one, focusing on contractual arrangements rather than on policy design and the creation of institutions.

In the 1960s and 1970s attention turned to the conceptual basis for the measurement of poverty and inequality, with a concentration on the income dimension. Income distribution was tracked in formal models. There was considerable discussion of the influence of income distribution on savings and growth and of how growth itself would influence income distribution. (Much of this discussion built on the work of Arthur Lewis and Simon Kuznets; see, for example, Lewis 1955; Kuznets 1971.) This period saw growing interest in the empirical study of poverty and income distribution.[5]

---

5. Robert McNamara, as president of the World Bank, made his famous Nairobi speech on income distribution and poverty in 1974.

The 1980s brought a shift in concerns, driven in part by availability of data and computing technology and in part by the poor results from statist policies that had led to slow growth, acute problems of structural adjustment and debt, or both. Much empirical work was done on structural adjustment. Toward the mid-1980s an increasing concern with theories of growth resurfaced—in part because of developments in the theory of industrial organization and in part as a result of empirical work that made use of large, newly available bodies of cross-country data, in particular the Penn studies of Kravis, Summers, and Heston (Kravis, Heston, and Summers 1982; Summers and Heston 1988, 1991). Empirical work with these macro data sets was aimed, among other things, at understanding what factors create a good incentive regime for efficient investment. Data, computing, and econometric advances allowed for the development of empirical studies using household survey data. These data sets were multipurpose and were applied to models of individual and household behavior, as well as to the evaluation of the consequences of different policies for income distributions and standards of living.

Research in the 1990s, including that at the World Bank, shifted to focus on the role of institutions in development. The importance of institutions such as those associated with the rule of law and the financial system has been established. There has also been growing work on the political economy of policy reform and of institution-building. Social cohesion is now seen as an important foundation for sound policies and institutions (Easterly and Levine 1997).

The term social capital has been used fairly generally to cover norms, associations, and networks that influence how individuals and communities react to different kinds of incentives and opportunities. At the most basic level, recognizing its absence can help us understand the kind of looting that went on in the 1990s in some of the countries of the former Soviet Union. More constructively, we can see how poor people depend on their networks to create credit and share risks. At the community level innovative efforts have been made to measure social capital and demonstrate its importance for provision of local public services (Narayan and Pritchett 1999).

These strands of work laid a foundation for the reexamination of the role of foreign aid in development. Because progress in a number of countries has been held back more by poor institutions and policies than by lack of resources, the financing of "gaps" did not produce good results. Furthermore, policy change has turned out to be a complex social and political phenomenon, so that deeper thought is required than simply making assistance conditional on detailed policy measures. The success of some World Bank–supported reform programs has depended more on underlying political-economy factors than on the efforts of the Bank or of other outside actors (Dollar and Svensson 2000). Thus, this reexamination concludes that aid can be a critical support to communities and countries in which there is a genuine movement for change but that the country must be "in the driver's seat" if reform programs are to succeed.

Looking to the future, we have to go beyond recognition of the importance of institutions and ask how to create effective institutions for development. Similarly, on social capital, we must ask how it is determined and whether there are any policies or interventions that will help build it.

Agenda for Action and Research

The nature of the policy problems facing developing countries has changed in the past decade, partly because of external factors (such as international capital flows) but mostly because these countries have made progress in macroeconomic and trade reforms and have moved on to a more complex set of issues. In the 1980s we could advise countries to stabilize and open up to trade and suggest how to do it. Reform programs were broadly similar along these dimensions, and the advice was largely sound.

The analogous advice to countries today is: improve your investment climate, ensure participation of the poor (health and education, vital in their own right, will be key to this participation), and provide poor people with some protection from dislocation and risk. In these areas one can offer generalized advice—for example, on the importance of sound tax regimes and tax administration and of reducing corruption and improving the investment climate. But the specifics are of great importance. Governments need to diagnose where, specifically, their problems lie, to design and build institutions and programs to address the weaknesses, and to get continuous feedback on whether services are improving.

Investment Climate

In the area of investment climate, there is no substitute for systematic information from firms. All the industrial countries conduct enterprise surveys, but even in the more advanced developing countries it is rare for the government to survey firms systematically. Informal consultations are useful too, but they risk giving excessive weight to large firms and existing industries, whereas small and medium-size enterprises (SMEs) and new industries will be important for future growth. Good surveys steer away from the opinions of business people, and focus on the facts: How long does it take to clear goods from customs? How frequent are power outages? What are the costs of telecommunications, power, and transport services? How many different permits and licenses are required for the business to function? How much has to be paid in bribes for different decisions? This kind of information is necessary in order to identify the key bottlenecks in the investment climate. Comparison of this information across countries is extremely revealing and is often useful in galvanizing support for change.

Typically, the key problems of the investment climate will vary from country to country (and from region to region within a country). In one place the bottleneck will be the weeks it takes to clear customs; in another it will be unreliable power. In most cases, the underlying problem will be an institutional failure involving, for example, corruption or inefficient regulation or poor incentives in the public sector, and the solution will require the design of new institutional arrangements with proper incentives and monitoring, together with regular feedback mechanisms. We must include among the problems here the norms of behavior of both public officials and private agents. Indeed, of great importance in future research will be examination of the interactions between policy reforms, institutional change, and behavioral norms.

Participation of the Poor

We can make similar points concerning participation of the poor in development. The analysis starts with diagnosing the specific problems, which could be access to education, health, land, finance, or insurance mechanisms. In many cases, systematic individual and household surveys are needed to make the diagnosis. As with the investment climate, key obstacles are likely to stem from institutional problems—weak markets and weak organizational structures for land services or for small-scale credit, or ineffective provision of public services in poor communities. The solutions will involve designing, building, and fostering institutions that actually work.

The International Community

What is the role of the World Bank and the larger international community in supporting these efforts? We see this role as fourfold. First, the international community should provide finance to low-income countries that have embarked resolutely on the "first generation" reforms of macroeconomic adjustment and trade liberalization. Research has shown that financial aid can have a large impact on growth and poverty reduction in this context (Burnside and Dollar 2000). Donors have responded by making their aid allocations more selective in the past few years. The overall volume of aid, however, remains at historically low levels, and we would urge the rich countries to be more generous. We are suggesting that donors consider moving away from very detailed conditionality on a large range of policies (broadly, the current practice) and instead condition the level of aid on a few key policies for which there is clear evidence of effectiveness. We have learned that development assistance *can* deliver for the poor.

Second, the international community should support the provision of global or regional public goods. One interpretation of recent pressures on the international financial institutions (IFIs) is that there is a broad coalition in industrial and developing countries for poverty reduction. In this very constructive sense, poverty reduction is a global public good, and our recommendations address it. There are other public goods such as malaria control or an AIDS vaccine that would make big contributions to world welfare. Clearly, many of these global public goods are underfunded.

Third, we think that a development agency such as the World Bank can help countries with the process of diagnosis, institutional design, and feedback. The Bank has played a leading role in the development of household surveys to help with poverty analysis and the design of anti-poverty programs. One of our current initiatives in the Research Group is to help countries more systematically collect from firms information that is comparable across countries. This promises to be an invaluable diagnostic tool for assessing the investment climate and for helping design institutional and other improvements. Much of the Bank's detailed sectoral involvement is aimed at strengthening institutions that affect either the investment climate or the participation of the poor. We view the Bank's role in the diagnosis/design/feedback process as in large part a "knowledge" role that does not necessarily involve finance or conditionality. What the Bank can bring to the process is broad knowledge of what has been tried and what has worked in other countries. Countries and communities will need to tailor this knowledge to their own local situation. In so doing, it is important that different agents and agencies have a clear understanding of how their activities complement those of others on the key dimensions for action. That is a basic contribution of a Comprehensive Development Framework.

Fourth—and dear to the hearts of those of us in the Research Group— we think that the Bank, with its international perspective and experience, has a special responsibility and position for pursuing an active social science research agenda and linking this to efforts to strengthen research capacity in the developing world. It has enormous advantages over other institutions in carrying out comparative research programs; indeed it is uniquely placed to do so and to draw on the best conceptual and empirical ideas and researchers from around the world. Often, such research will require basic and creative examination of the underlying theoretical approaches.

Research is closely related to the process of diagnosis/design/feedback, but it is not the same thing. On some of the important new issues that emerged in the 1990s, it is difficult to make recommendations because both our conceptual and knowledge bases are limited. For example, we have gone beyond the mere recognition of the importance of institutions, but we are only in the early stages of understanding how to build them. Various pieces of research have shown that in ethnically diverse societies, the quality of public services tends to be low, and this suggests that there may be some important social capital that affects service provision. However, we are only beginning to examine what determines social capital or what institutional arrangements might mitigate the impact of low social capital.

We have identified in this paper a wide range of areas in which increasing knowledge could yield large practical benefits. If the World Bank is to fulfill the role of a knowledge partner helping communities with the process of diagnosis/design/feedback, then the effort will require a foundation in research. At the same time, success in that knowledge role will strengthen profoundly the Bank's ability to pursue research on issues at the cutting edge of development.

Building a Climate for Investment, Growth, and Poverty Reduction in India

Nicholas Stern

The Export-Import Bank of India, Mumbai, March 22, 2001

It is a great pleasure to be here at the Export-Import Bank of India to deliver the annual Commencement Day lecture. EXIM has long played a key role in India's ever-expanding presence on the world stage, and it surely has a major and growing agenda. I have followed India's progress for a long time, and I am deeply committed to this country. As a researcher, I lived and worked in the small Uttar Pradesh village of Palanpur during much of the agricultural year of 1974/75, and I have been able to return there on many occasions during the past 25 years. Seeing Palanpur grow and change has taught me much of what I know of development (Lanjouw & Stern 1998). The key drivers of its growth—which has been significant, if slow and haphazard—have been off-farm employment in small and medium-size firms and agricultural productivity. In the 1980s and 1990s I also studied economic policymaking at the central and state levels, and I observed how perceptions of the role of the private sector were changing. In this process, and in my work on rural India, I have formed a great admiration for Indian entrepreneurship across the board.

India's experience has, in many ways, embodied and driven change in development thinking. Its agenda has shifted from relatively statist and planned to more liberal and open. As has happened in other developing countries, India has generated positive results from its reforms. Indeed the main theme of my talk will be that by building on this progress and deepening these reforms, India now has a great opportunity to accelerate growth and poverty reduction.

The reform agenda that I am going to discuss can be brought together under the rubric of "improving the investment climate." Now that macroeconomic and trade reforms have been carried out (or are under way)

This speech was previously published in the EBRD's *The Economics of Transition*, volume 9, no. 2, 2001. The contributions of David Dollar and his team and of Peter Lanjouw were most valuable in preparing this lecture. I am also grateful for the contributions of Shahrokh Fardoust, Halsey Rogers, Hope Neighbor, and Oeindrila Dube.

and have borne fruit, the main question is, what other changes at a more institutional and micro level are needed to create a fertile climate for investment, productivity growth, and job creation?

I am optimistic that India is answering this question in a clear and constructive way. Today, I will discuss some concrete areas in which further progress would have a big payoff. To preface that discussion, I want to be very clear on two points. First, when I use the term "investment climate," I am speaking of the climate for rural as well as urban productivity and investment. Indeed, rural entrepreneurship is key to overcoming poverty in India. Second, the fight against poverty cannot be waged through the investment climate alone. We must also work to empower poor people and invest in them to ensure that they are able to be fully involved in both the process of growth and the rewards from growth. Although I shall have something to say on both topics today, the empowerment story must be the subject of another lecture.

In trying to answer the question that I posed a moment ago, I shall make four broad points:

- Globalization has created great opportunities for India, which it is embracing only in part.

- The central challenge in reaping greater benefits from globalization lies in improving the investment climate—that is, in providing sound regulation of industry, including the promotion of competition; in overcoming bureaucratic delay and inefficiency; in fighting corruption; and in improving the quality of infrastructure.

- While the investment climate is clearly important for large, formal sector firms, it is just as important—if not more so—for small and medium-size enterprises (SMEs), the informal sector, agricultural productivity, and the generation of off-farm employment. For these reasons, the investment climate is itself a key issue for poverty reduction.

- There are large variations across Indian states in the quality of the investment climate and the strength of reforms, and the states with a positive climate are experiencing more rapid growth and faster reduction of poverty. The challenge for lagging states is to learn from the experience of the first group.

These points involve mostly structural and micro issues. In examining the micro issues, I will be drawing on collaborative research involving

World Bank and Indian researchers and on comparisons of these results across the states of India. The analysis points to the kind of policy reforms that can provide India with a much more positive investment climate and foster growth in output.

Globalization and the Developing Countries

I am going to say only a few words about my first point, concerning the opportunities from globalization, because it is, I believe, the least controversial. What I mean by globalization is the growing economic integration among nations, reflected in larger flows of trade, services, foreign investment, people, and information. We should note that these same processes can also bring crime, conflict, disease, and instability. But it is pointless to think that the integrative forces can be reversed; the challenge is to make the most of them while mitigating the risks.

The sources of this integration lie in part in technological innovations. But integration has also been driven by a clear policy choice by many developing countries, based on their own analysis of their experience and that of others, to participate more in the global economy by lowering trade and investment barriers. It has been, for the most part, a sound choice based on sound analysis.

The two most populous countries in the world, India and China, are the most striking and important examples of this shift in policy toward openness. In India's case the early five-year plans were very much focused on state-led, inward-oriented development. But what India and other developing countries have found is that while the state-led model can generate fairly high investment rates and capital accumulation, it has not succeeded in stimulating the sustained productivity growth that is the hallmark of long-run economic development in the most advanced economies. Something that constantly reminded me of this on my many visits to India was the fact that the ever-present Ambassador was the same model of car, the Morris Oxford, that I had known as a child in the United Kingdom in the 1950s.

In the three decades beginning in 1950, China closed its face to the outside world even more emphatically than did India. Through high investment in education and physical capital, it managed to grow more rapidly than India, despite suffering the traumas of the Great Leap Forward and famine in the years around 1960, as well as the Cultural Revolution of the late 1960s and early 1970s. The experience of India and

China does show that the state-led model can, for a while, generate accumulation-driven growth. But the model is inefficient and undynamic.

China and India, each in its own way, drew their conclusions from the experience of the three decades from 1950 on. The single most important development in the world economy in the past 20 years has been the shift of these two countries toward more outward-oriented development strategies and the freeing of entrepreneurial spirits. Both economies have found that significant and positive results have flowed from reform. India's average annual growth rate of real per capita income rose from about 1 percent in the 1970s to almost 4 percent in the 1980s and 1990s, and China's per capita income growth rate accelerated from about 2 percent in the 1960s to almost 3 percent in the 1970s and then 9 percent in the 1980s and the 1990s. This trend is all the more remarkable because what happened to the growth rate of the high-income countries as a group has been exactly the opposite; according to World Bank data, their per capita growth slowed steadily from 4.5 percent in the 1960s to 1.6 percent in the 1990s (see Figure 1). Thus, between

Figure 1. Growth Rates of Real Per Capita Gross Domestic Product (GDP): China, India, and High-Income Countries, 1960s–1990s

Annual average

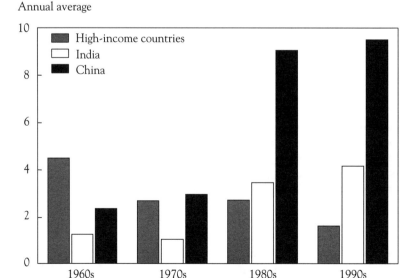

Source: World Bank data.

1960 and 1980 India and China were falling further and further behind the advanced economies, but since 1980 they have begun to catch up.

Now, while India has done reasonably well with its reform program, one point that is striking is that it has attracted so little foreign investment. Benefits can come from many types of integration—from expanded trade and greater Internet use, for example—but one important vehicle for these benefits is foreign direct investment (FDI). Both the macro and the micro evidence suggest that this is an important conduit for new technology, as well as for management experience and access to markets. Indeed it was foreign investment from Suzuki that finally introduced to India a genuinely new car, which quickly became the largest-selling model.

Foreign investment has been going primarily to the large reforming economies. In 1998, World Bank data show, China received FDI amounting to 5 percent of gross domestic product (GDP). The corresponding figures were 4 percent for Brazil, 2.5 percent for Mexico—and, for India, less than half of 1 percent. In other words, China, with a GDP twice that of India, received 20 times as much FDI (CII 2000). This and other evidence suggests that India is not benefiting as much from globalization as it could—which leads me to my second point.

What Makes for a Good Investment Climate?

The quantity and quality of investment in India or in any other developing country depend on the returns that investors expect and the uncertainties around those returns. It is useful to think of three broad and interrelated components that shape these expectations: the macroeconomic situation, governance, and infrastructure.

Macroeconomic issues. First are macroeconomic or country-level issues concerning economic and political stability and nationwide policy toward foreign trade and investment. Here, India looks good; in fact, it is these macro-level reforms that in large measure drove the high growth of the 1990s. Relative macroeconomic and political stability, and trade liberalization with further commitments within the World Trade Organization (WTO)—these make up one crucial set of ingredients for spurring investment and productivity growth.

But creating a good climate for investment involves two other factors as well: the institutions of economic governance, and the foundation of basic infrastructure (power, transport, telecommunications, and so on).

It is common for developing countries to start with the macro reforms, which often produce good results compared with past performance. If, however, the country does not move ahead on the institutional and infrastructure agenda, the growth generated by macro reform is likely to peter out. I think it is now broadly recognized within India that the country has reached a crucial point and that the challenge now is to move forward on this institutional and infrastructure agenda.

It is instructive to look at *The Competitiveness Yearbook* to put India in an international context on these matters. The yearbook (International Institute for Management Development 2000) ranks 47 countries—basically, the members of the Organisation for Economic Co-operation and Development (OECD), plus emerging market economies—on a range of factors, with the top performer ranked 1. The rankings are based on the opinions of 3,000 executives. Of the 47 countries, India ranks 43rd overall, while China is 31st (Figure 2). India scores very well on such measures as its supply of skilled workers, in which it ranks 12th. It does less well in those areas identified in the survey as particularly important for reform, which are key elements of a good investment

Figure 2. Competitiveness Rankings, China and India, 2000
(country rankings, 1–47, with 47 best)

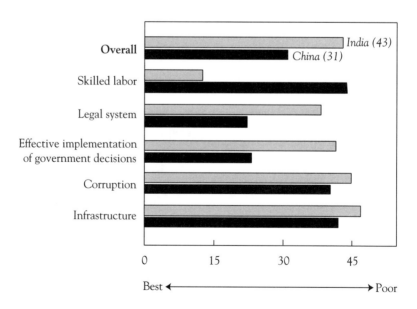

Source: Based on International Institute for Management Development 2000.

climate: curbing corruption (ranked 45th), improving the effective implementation of government policies (42nd), and infrastructure (47th). The foreign investment numbers cited earlier indicate that businesses are acting on these perceptions.

Governance. Turning to the governance component of the investment climate, let me take the institutional questions first. Obviously, all countries need to regulate firms in some ways—for example, on fire, safety, pollution, and monopolistic practices. This is true for every market economy. The issues are the extent and nature of regulation, its effectiveness and transparency, and the corruption associated with it. The evidence shows great variation across developing countries. To take one example, according to the World Business Environment Survey, which covers a large range of countries, managers report spending about 5 percent of their time dealing with government officials in Latin American countries and about twice that in the transition economies of Eastern Europe, many of which are well known for bureaucracy and corruption (World Bank 2000f). For India the average reported in the survey was 16 percent of management time. Those who have worked in India know that it can indeed be very difficult to get things done. Bureaucratic harassment can be an art form, a special consumption good that too many bureaucrats enjoy—money does not have to change hands to realize the psychic fulfillment of ritual humiliation. (Having said that, let me also say that some of the individuals and friends I admire most in the world serve in India's administration.)

Two other related areas of regulation that I want to single out concern the exit or bankruptcy of firms and the redundancy of labor. India's bankruptcy and liquidation procedures are notoriously cumbersome, with recent estimates showing that over 60 percent of liquidation cases before the High Courts have been in process for more than 10 years (Mathur 1993). The burden on SMEs regarding labor redundancies has been recognized and is addressed in the new budget, with proposals that the size ceiling beneath which firms are not required to seek government permission to retrench workers be raised from 100 to 1,000 employees. These areas of regulation are of great importance, because much of the productivity growth that comes from a more open and competitive economy arises from the movement of capital and labor from less-productive to more-productive activities. If regulations make it difficult for labor and capital to adjust, much of the potential benefit of openness is lost. I should, however, make it clear that the argument is not antilabor; workers' rights are of great importance. Rather, it is in favor of productive employment and growth.

Let me give you a concrete example. A recent study of the Indian machine tool industry by John Sutton of the London School of Economics found that some Indian firms were very competitive in the production of computer numerically controlled (CNC) lathes (Sutton 2000). When Sutton compared the Indian firms with best practice in Taiwan (China) and in Japan, he found that the real productivity of the best Indian firms had improved in the face of new international competition. Their productivity was now close to the level in Taiwan, whose firms are leaders in the world market for this product. Since the wages for the skilled labor used in this field are six times higher in Taiwan, the best Indian firms are very competitive, domestically and internationally. Sutton also found, however, huge variations in productivity among Indian producers—much more so than among Taiwanese firms.

This is a common feature of heavily regulated, closed economies: large productivity differences among firms producing the same thing. With a more open strategy, what we would expect to happen in this industry is some shake-out, with more successful firms expanding and perhaps taking over some competitors and with, probably, some firms going out of business. I recognize that there are real social costs involved in these adjustments and that it is important to have good social protection policies to help workers, in particular, adjust. But the key word here is adjustment. If regulations make it difficult for firms to reshape their labor forces or to enter or exit when necessary, the benefits from globalization will be severely constrained. Sutton also notes that in the altered situation created by the opening of the machine tool industry to greater foreign competition, it is a new firm that is the top Indian performer and that is growing most rapidly.

Not only does heavy regulation of labor relations and of firm entry and exit make it difficult for existing Indian firms to compete; these regulations must be one of the prime reasons why India has seen so much less foreign investment than other large reforming economies. The procedural hurdles faced by prospective foreign investors provide a striking example. The Confederation of Indian Industry (CII) reports that a typical power project needs to obtain 43 clearances at the central government level and 57 at the state level. For mining projects the numbers are 37 and 47. One result is that, cumulatively, only a quarter of approved foreign investments was actually realized between 1991 and 1999 (Ministry of Industry 1999). But I am not arguing for special privileges for foreign investment. The priority is to generate the productivity and investment that will be required for sustained growth, and these will be driven first and foremost by Indian firms. What is good for Indian enterprises is good for foreign investment, as well. Foreign investors need no special privileges, and there is no need to offer such inducements. It is the investment climate that counts.

Infrastructure. Infrastructure is the third broad investment climate issue. The shortcomings of the power supply in India are well known. Although this problem is a deterrent for big investors, many of them would expect to have their own generators anyway. It is SMEs that are especially burdened by the unreliable power supply.

One of our important projects in the Research Group of the World Bank has been to work with the Confederation of Indian Industry on a survey of 1,000 manufacturing and software firms in 10 Indian states (CII and World Bank 2001). We have conducted similar surveys on the investment climate in other countries as well. India is fairly remarkable in that most of the SMEs we surveyed had their own power generators, something that is much less common in, say, the Republic of Korea or Thailand (Hallward-Driemeier 2001). To have a vibrant SME sector, a functioning public power grid is needed. One of the positive things about large-scale foreign investment is that many multinational firms like to develop a set of local parts suppliers, and this is a great stimulus to the SME sector. But if the basic economic infrastructure is poor, the country receives less foreign investment, and there is less spillover benefit to SMEs from the investment it does attract.

One other infrastructure issue I want to mention is the operation of seaports. Here, governance and infrastructure intersect. Governance is important because international trade has to pass through customs. We have found in our surveys that Indian firms report an average time for clearing goods from customs that is about twice as high as in emerging markets such as Korea or Thailand and three to four times as high as in Singapore or the most efficient OECD countries. Furthermore, there is a lot of variation in how long it takes. For any firm, this delay and the variation in it impose a high, tax-like cost. A firm needs to keep larger inventories to protect against these delays, and holding inventories costs money. And in India, the cost of credit is particularly high.

Aside from customs clearance, there is the issue of how well ports operate. Inefficient ports combine with transport costs to make countries less competitive. As Figure 3 shows, sending an identical shipment of textiles to the United States from India costs, on average, 20 percent more than from Thailand and 35 percent more than from China.

Figure 3. Cost Savings in Maritime Transport of a Shipment of Textiles to the United States from Selected Countries Compared with India

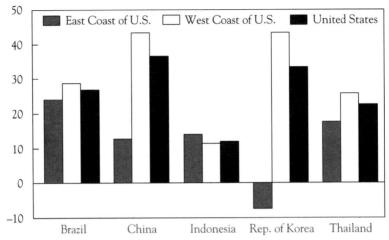

Percent

Source: U.S. Department of Transportation, U.S. Import Waterborne Databank.

The Investment Climate and Poverty Reduction

My third point is that the investment climate plays a crucial role in poverty reduction. When developing countries improve their investment climates, the poor benefit. How do they gain?

First, some members of poor households obtain employment from formal sector firms that expand in a good investment climate. The poor are more likely to be employed in small and medium-size formal sector firms than in the very largest firms, which are able to select the most educated and most skilled workers. My own experience of studying economic diversification in Palanpur village, Uttar Pradesh, has indicated that employment in SMEs is occasionally within the reach of even the very poor in rural areas, although it must be recognized that the better educated and better connected often have an advantage in gaining such jobs. Given adequate transport infrastructure (in the case of Palanpur, a railway link to the nearby towns of Moradabad and Chandausi), employment in bakeries, metal-polishing shops, textile mills, and other factories is not only possible but is highly valued by farm households seeking to balance their portfolio of activities (Lanjouw and Stern 1998). I have already noted that the problems of bureaucracy, corruption, and poor infrastructure take their greatest toll on this SME sector. Large firms are often able to find ways around bureaucratic and public infrastructure problems, but small firms have fewer options. We found in our survey with the CII that the impact of a poor investment climate on firm productivity was greater for SMEs than for large firms.

Second, a positive investment climate has benefits for the informal sectors, which is where the poor often have the best chance of finding employment. Formal sector employment creates new demand for informal sector expansion, as well as for more farm output at better prices. Increases in agricultural productivity and farm income, in turn, generate additional off-farm employment opportunities. Off-farm employment is crucial in combating rural poverty. Let us look at some of the evidence on these points from India.

Research carried out by the World Bank in collaboration with the National Council for Applied Economic Research (NCAER) in Delhi shows that in 1994 roughly a third of household income in rural areas in India accrued from nonfarm sources (Lanjouw and Shariff 2000). This countrywide average masks considerable variation across states, a point to which I will return. The nonfarm incomes come from a variety of sectors, including commerce, manufacturing, and services, and stem from regular and part-time wage employment, as well as from own-enterprise activities. Evidence from village studies documents that rural households value such nonfarm incomes highly, not only because they contribute significantly to overall income levels but also because they can reduce the exposure of households to potentially devastating income fluctuations stemming from harvest variability.

Rising nonfarm incomes are associated with increased demand and higher prices for cash crops such as fruits and vegetables. In addition, to the extent that the nonfarm sector can provide farm households with a stable source of income, farmers move closer to crop choices that maximize expected profit rather than minimize risk.

Although there is evidence that even the poor sometimes do find employment in the nonfarm economy, they more typically lack the assets, particularly the educational levels, necessary to gain access to such jobs. The World Bank–NCAER study indicates that the poor also often face other barriers associated with low social status and low wealth. These findings resonate with my observations for Palanpur, where access to regular nonfarm employment depends critically on a network of contacts who can provide information about vacancies and who may be able to furnish references. It is generally the higher-status households that have access to such networks. In addition, villagers in Palanpur are often required to pay bribes to obtain the more attractive nonfarm jobs. As a result the poor are generally confined to casual employment in unskilled nonfarm activities or engage in residual, last-resort, self-employment activities. This emphasizes the point I made at the outset: improving the investment climate is crucial to poverty reduction, but it is far from the whole story. We also have to empower and invest in poor people if they are to play a full part in the growth process and overcome poverty (Lanjouw and Stern 1998).

Research undertaken in the World Bank by Martin Ravallion and Gaurav Datt illustrates how these mechanisms fit into an aggregate picture of economic performance across Indian states (Ravallion and Datt 1999).[1] The authors show that in the period from 1960 to 1994 the pace of poverty reduction varied widely across states. The contribution to poverty reduction of farm productivity and development spending did not typically vary much by state, but the impact of nonfarm growth did vary markedly. Those states with initially higher farm productivity, a smaller gap between rural and urban living standards, and better educational levels experienced growth that was clearly more pro-poor. Basic education was especially important in explaining why nonfarm growth had more of an effect on poverty in some states than in others. The sectoral composition of growth (notably, how much comes from agriculture) is key, especially in states with low human resource development. Let me reiterate: the investment climate—the three dimensions that I have emphasized being stability and openness, governance, and infrastructure—is as important to those investing in their farms and agricultural activities as it is to those investing elsewhere.

It is of some comfort to note that even when the poor do not yet enjoy easy access to nonfarm employment opportunities, expansion of the nonfarm sector can still contribute to poverty reduction. As is shown by the World Bank–NCAER study, growth in nonfarm employment is often associated with rising agricultural wage rates. The study indicates that this effect is particularly strong in the construction sector, where increases in construction employment lead to a tightening of the agri-

---

1. See "The India Poverty Project: Poverty and Growth in India, 1952–1994," http://www.worldbank.org/poverty/data/indiapaper.htm.

cultural labor market, resulting in higher agricultural wages. A well-known stylized fact about rural poverty in India is that agricultural laborers are highly represented among the rural poor in most parts of the country. With more than 250 million people, accounting for over two-thirds of India's entire labor force, still employed in agriculture, it is clear that an expanding nonfarm sector which exerts upward pressure on agricultural wages can play a crucial role in aggregate poverty reduction, even via this indirect route (Lanjouw and Shariff 2000).

In India expansion of the nonfarm sector has been steady, with the share of nonfarm employment rising from around 19 percent in the 1970s to around 24 percent in 1997 (Acharya and Mitra 2000). In Palanpur I witnessed this process firsthand. While the village economy remains primarily oriented toward agriculture, employment in regular and semiregular nonfarm jobs has increased dramatically, both in number and in range of activities, since the 1950s, resulting in a contribution to village income (depending on the quality of the harvest) of more than one-third (Lanjouw and Stern 1998).

This expansion of nonfarm employment in India is welcome, but it is slower and more uneven than might be hoped. In China nonfarm enterprises grew at a rapid rate after liberalization policies were introduced in the late 1970s and early 1980s, first in agriculture and then elsewhere. China's annual rate of growth of off-farm employment over the past 20 years or so has been 12 percent, versus the 2 percent observed in India.

To a considerable extent, India's slower progress in this regard can be attributed to the development strategy it has pursued. A large share of total nonfarm investment in India has been directed to public works projects, especially during the 1980s. These projects often combine the provision of infrastructure with a safety net for the poor in the form of jobs. Their importance in mitigating poverty has been widely noted.

Sustaining these expenditures during the 1990s has been difficult, in the face of fiscal constraints, and this has led to a slowdown of public investment–induced poverty reduction in recent years. Yet employment-generating projects are surely much more important than deeply wasteful subsidies, such as those in infrastructure—power, in particular—or for fertilizers.

Public works projects have also played a role in China, and what has been particularly noteworthy is the extent to which such infrastructure provision has been accompanied by a pro–rural industry investment climate that has made possible a major expansion of rural nonfarm employment. Today, an estimated 31 percent of the rural labor force in China is employed in rural industry, compared with 18 percent in India (Lele, Gandhi, and Gautum 2001). Rural enterprises in China have been both a major engine of economic growth and a potent force for rural poverty reduction during the past two decades.

To summarize the conclusions from the examination of this third point, and to underline a key part of what I want to say today, great potential exists in India for improvements in investment climate that can translate into further progress in poverty reduction. An expansion of both formal and informal nonfarm employment, particularly in rural areas and in the small urban centers that service them, can provide highly sought after employment to the poor. Such an expansion can also tighten labor markets in general, allowing even those who remain employed in agriculture to benefit. The injection of nonfarm incomes into rural areas will also boost agriculture and kick off further rounds of linkages. To the extent that the improved investment climate is accompanied by policies to improve the capacity of the poor to participate in the nonfarm sector (education will be central here), there are grounds for expecting India's performance in poverty reduction to at least match that of China.

Variations in the Investment Climate among Indian States

The last point that I want to take up in this analysis is the large variation in the investment climate across Indian states. India's national-level reform is yielding its greatest benefits in states that are complementing that reform with improvements in the investment climate at the micro level.

Gaining insights into the impact of the differences in state-level investment climates was a key motivation for undertaking the 1,000 firm survey with the CII. The survey covered 10 Indian states. Among other questions, we asked entrepreneurs to identify the states with the best investment climates and to estimate the cost saving from operating in these locations relative to the states with the worst climates. I recognize that this is subjective, but it is a starting point for looking at differences in the investment climate.

In the first place, we found fairly consistent views. Delhi was roughly in the middle, making it a useful reference point. The entrepreneurs viewed Maharashtra, Karnataka, Gujarat, Tamil Nadu, and Andhra

Figure 4. Cost Advantage in Relation to Delhi, 10 Indian States

Percent

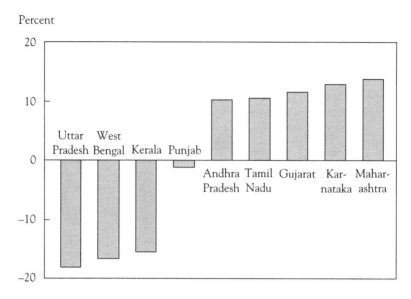

Source: CII and World Bank 2001.

Pradesh as better places to produce than Delhi, whereas Punjab, Kerala, West Bengal, and Uttar Pradesh were perceived to be worse (see Figure 4). The estimated cost difference between the best and the worst states was about 30 percent, which is a very large hurdle for the poor-policy states to overcome in trying to attract investment.

A second important finding was that the objective data on productivity closely match these subjective views; entrepreneurs, even in small firms, are pretty well informed about variations in problems and bottlenecks. So, in the same sector and controlling for size, we find that firms in the good-climate states have about 30 percent more value added per worker than do firms in poor-climate states. One point that I find very interesting is that capital per worker is actually somewhat higher in the poor-climate states. This makes sense to me because a firm operating in the poor-climate environments, is, for example, more likely to need its own generator—a large capital outlay.

The good-climate states have higher wages, a finding that we will examine more closely in our research. Perhaps this reflects the use of higher-quality (that is, more educated or more experienced) labor as better workers migrate to the good production locations. Or it may reflect

Figure 5. Productivity Gaps between States with Good and Poor Investment Climates, by Source of Productivity, India

Proportionate gap in relation to Delhi (percent)

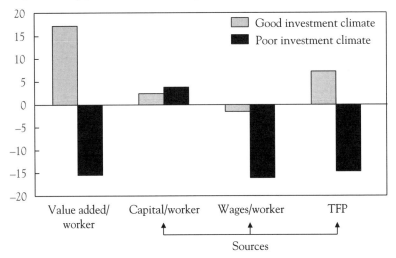

Note: TFP, Total factor productivity.
Source: CII and World Bank 2001.

higher payments for the same skills in good-climate states, which would indicate that some of the productivity gain from the better climate is being passed through to the workers. Probably both explanations are relevant. The CII and the World Bank have recently produced a comprehensive report, "Improving the Investment Climate in India," on the basis of this survey and other information.

Firms in the good-climate states have higher total factor productivity, which is basically a measure of how well capital and labor are being combined to produce value. We can trace these productivity differences back to specific problems in the investment climate. Some of the poor-climate states have particularly acute problems with the public power grid. In Uttar Pradesh 98 percent of the firms we surveyed had their own generators, and collectively the firms in the survey got only 50 percent of their power from the public grid. In Maharashtra, by contrast, only 44 percent of the firms had their own generators, and taken together, the firms drew 90 percent of their power from the public grid. I want to emphasize again what a burden an uncertain power supply imposes on a small firm, for which own–power generation is extremely costly and capital-intensive.

The regulatory burden of government also varies by state. The number of times per year that firms are visited by government officials is more than twice as high in the poor-climate states as in the good-climate states.

Naturally, these differences translate into differences in the rates of investment and growth across states. For our sample of firms, the average real growth rate of sales for the past five years was 9 percent per year in the good-climate states but only 2 percent in the poor-climate ones. The aggregate growth figures for these states are quite consistent with this pattern.

Let me close by linking my last two points: the investment climate varies across Indian states, and better investment climates lead to more rapid poverty reduction. The combination of open policies at the national level and good governance and infrastructure at the micro level have delivered on the poverty reduction agenda in the 1990s; the available data suggest that the good-climate states as a group reduced poverty at considerably faster rates than the poor-climate states.

Conclusions

When I give a talk that focuses on the investment climate, there is a danger that I will be misperceived as a champion of big business and misunderstood as arguing that the investment climate agenda is all that is needed for poverty reduction. That is not what I am saying. There is an equally important agenda having to do with the issues of educating and empowering poor people, especially in rural areas, and assisting them to participate in the market economy. I have written and spoken extensively on that agenda and will have much to say about it going forward. Indeed, it was a central argument in *World Development Report 2000/2001: Attacking Poverty*.

That agenda of empowerment and education will have much greater impact if it is pursued simultaneously with the kinds of reforms of the investment climate that I have discussed here today. By the same token, reforms in the investment climate will be much more effective if the population is rapidly becoming more educated, more empowered, and better able to participate in the market economy.

I think that there is a tendency in some quarters to think of the investment climate agenda as being concerned with growth and the empowerment/education/rural development agenda as being concerned with distribution and poverty reduction. The former is taken as structural and the latter as social. That is the wrong way to think about how these two agendas interact. Improving the investment climate has as much of an effect on poverty reduction as any action directly aimed at poverty. In many real-world cases, improving the investment climate will be the single most important thing that can be done to alleviate mass poverty.

At the same time, enabling poor people to gain education and assisting them to obtain the assets and tools to participate in the market economy are not just measures for poverty reduction; they are also crucial for the growth of the whole economy. Rapid success in poverty reduction requires real progress on both the investment climate and the empowerment of poor people. I believe that India is making such progress and that it must continue to move forward. If it does, the next two decades will see great strides in poverty reduction. A halving of income poverty rates in India over the next 15 years is perfectly attainable. That would be a wonderful prize, for India and for the world.

Globalization, Reform, and Poverty Reduction: The Challenge and Implications for Indonesia

Nicholas Stern

Institute of Economic and Social Research, Faculty of Economics, University of Indonesia, December 15, 2000

The last decade of the twentieth century saw a remarkable acceleration in the pace of globalization. By globalization, I mean the growing integration of economies and societies through the flow between countries of information, ideas, activities, technologies, goods, services, capital, and people. The history of Indonesia, which has been a crossroads of peoples and cultures for many centuries, teaches us clearly that globalization is not a new phenomenon. And it is also true that globalization has ebbed and flowed in different periods; for example, it reached a high point in the early part of the twentieth century, only to decline as war and depression caused countries to retreat from world markets. Nevertheless, in the past decade we have seen not just another surge of globalization but truly extraordinary changes, particularly in communications technologies, of which the Internet is the most visible.

The improved flow of information alone would have had a dramatic effect on economies and societies. But the communications revolution has also been accompanied by declines in transport costs and by more open policies toward international trade and capital flows. The result is a much more integrated world economy than we had just 10 years ago. Capital flows have increased dramatically in the past decade, and trade has grown much faster than incomes. In *Global Economic Prospects 2001* the World Bank estimated that world trade volumes would increase by 12.5 percent in 2000, the most rapid rate of growth since before the oil shock of 1973.

The main theme of my talk will be that increased integration offers tremendous opportunities to developing countries but that it also carries with it serious risks. I will argue that with the right policies and institutions, the benefits from grasping the opportunities vastly outweigh the potential risks and costs. In establishing these policies and institutions, however, we must pay very close attention to the analysis of risks and to the costs of adjustment.

The risks and costs are of different types. Without the right policies and institutions, there can be great volatility, with large swings in income. This potential volatility clearly feeds the fears of many people around the world who are challenging globalization. Their fears go beyond concern over income. Many of those opposed to the growing integration worry about its effects on culture, the environment, disease, movement of people, and crime and violence, as well as about loss of control over their own lives. Although many of these fears and anxieties are understandable, we must recognize that key aspects of globalization are essentially irreversible, particularly those associated with information, ideas, and communications. This irreversibility, and the magnitude of the potential benefits, surely tell us that the central question is how to manage and gain from the process, not how to reject it.

Today, I would like to take stock of what we know about the impact of globalization—its impact both on developing countries generally and on poverty in particular, since that is the focus of the World Bank's work. In my assessment, I will emphasize four points:

- Globalization is, on the whole, a positive force for development and poverty reduction, although there are specific measures that the rich countries could take to make it much more favorable to development.

- To realize the great potential from globalization, countries need complementary institutions and policies.

- These institutions and policies can themselves be strengthened through countries' involvement in international markets. This prospect immediately raises issues of sequencing—which kinds of opening to undertake first in order to minimize the risks associated with globalization.

- Finally, there are specific measures that countries can take to ensure that poor people participate in globalization and benefit from it.

Globalization as a Positive Force for Development

There are sharp contrasts between countries in many of the dimensions of integration that I mentioned above. An example is the degree to which countries have embraced the Internet and open communication: more than 30 percent of the population in the United States has access to the Internet, but in the Middle East and North Africa, Latin

America, Africa, Asia, and Eastern Europe only 1 to 2 percent of the population enjoys the same service. Developing countries, many of which 20 years ago had quite restrictive policies toward foreign trade and investment, have opened up to the global market to very different extents. These differences across countries provide evidence for our examination of the impact of globalization on development.

Country Experiences: China, India, and Other Globalizers

The evidence from the two most populous countries, China and India, is of particular importance; both countries have chosen to become much more open to foreign trade and investment in the past two decades. There are other significant examples of countries moving strongly to open their economies that I would highlight as well: in Asia, the countries of the Association of Southeast Asian Nations (ASEAN), including Indonesia; in Latin America, Argentina and Mexico; in Eastern Europe, Hungary and Poland; and in Africa, Ghana and Uganda.

Growth rates for these recent globalizers have generally accelerated as the countries have become more open. This trend is clearest for China and India. These are the two countries with which I have been most involved personally in my research and policy work as a development economist. Their combined population accounts for more than one-third of the world's total and is more than two-fifths of the population of the developing countries as a group. The growth of their aggregate per capita income accelerated from roughly 2 percent in the 1970s to 3 percent in the 1980s and 5 percent in the 1990s. This acceleration is all the more remarkable because the growth rates of the rich countries slowed over this period, from 3 to 2.5 to 2 percent. Many of the other globalizers have seen their growth rates accelerate as well; Mexico, Uganda, and Vietnam are examples.

So in the 1990s, for the first time, the majority of the population of the developing world was living in economies that were growing distinctly faster than the member economies of the Organisation for Economic Co-operation and Development (OECD)—that is, they were catching up. One of the distinctive features of those developing economies that did well was their greater participation in trade and investment. Conversely, in the large number of countries that had poor growth, or a decline, in incomes in the 1990s—countries such as Pakistan, Nigeria, and some of the former Soviet republics—trade and investment were not increasing.

The Responsibilities of the Rich Countries and the International Community

Clearly, as this evidence shows, integration with the international market can be effective in helping to increase incomes. However, the fact that some countries have had success with this path should not blind us to the possibility that the international trade and investment regime could be made much more favorable to development. Let me focus on three areas in which the rich countries, and the international community at large, could take steps to increase the development returns to trade liberalization: trade barriers, international standards, and intellectual property rights.

Trade barriers. Even after the Uruguay Round of trade liberalization, OECD countries still maintain significant barriers to trade from developing countries. Average tariffs in the United States, Canada, the European Union, and Japan—the "Quad" economies—range from only 4.3 percent in Japan to 8.3 percent in Canada, but their tariffs and trade barriers are much higher on many products exported by developing countries. Products subject to high tariffs in Quad countries include major agricultural staple food products such as meat, sugar, and dairy products, where tariff rates frequently exceed 100 percent; fruits and vegetables, such as the bananas that are hit with a 180 percent tariff by the European Union once they exceed quotas; and textiles, clothing, and footwear, where tariff rates are in the 15 to 30 percent range for many products. All these are sectors in which developing countries have a comparative advantage.

In the World Bank's latest research on trade, we estimated that the tariff and nontariff barriers imposed by rich countries, together with the agricultural subsidies that they give their farmers, cost developing countries much more than the $50 billion or so that these countries receive in foreign aid every year. We at the World Bank see this as one of the most important contributions that industrial countries could make to development: the abolition, once and for all, of the trade barriers and subsidies that prevent developing country products from reaching their markets. It is surely hypocritical of rich countries to encourage poor countries to liberalize trade and to tackle the associated problems of adjustment while at the same time succumbing to powerful groups in their own countries that seek to perpetuate protection of their narrow self-interest. Such protection damages both the economies of the rich countries themselves and the economies of the poor countries whose development they profess to support.

Environmental and labor standards. Various types of standards being proposed for inclusion in the World Trade Organization (WTO) framework—notably, environmental and labor standards—could become new vehicles for industrial country protectionism. Take the case of child labor. There can surely be no doubting the importance of children attending school and receiving a good education instead of being in the labor market. Indeed, education is at once a central objective of development, an end in itself, and a potent force for raising incomes—which is why it is a key priority in the work of the World Bank. But if we try to tackle the child labor problem through the WTO, there is a real danger that interest groups from wealthy countries will essentially tie up poor countries in court over this issue. The result would be less trade and less development—and, as a result, probably more child labor.

In contrast to the negative approach of trade sanctions, let us look to more positive means. Parents send young children to work when they are poor and lack other options. Bangladesh has tried to attack the root causes of child labor and poverty traps through its Food for Education program, which provides food subsidies to poor families that send their children to school. This program has succeeded in cutting child labor in half in communities where it has been implemented. The District Primary Education Programme, recently implemented in India with support from the World Bank, now covers 55 million children. Under this program, India has seen dramatic increases both in school attendance of children, particularly girls, and in the quality of education. The point is that if we care about child labor, there are constructive programs we can support—but they do require resources. If rich countries are serious about the child labor issue, they should support these programs. Sanctions levied through the WTO are not a productive substitute.

Intellectual property rights. At the moment, developing countries participating in the WTO are expected to adopt a standard set of laws on intellectual property protection. This is an area where I really doubt that one size fits all. Among the key recommendations of the recent U.K. White Paper on globalization is a proposal for a new Commission on Intellectual Property Rights to "examine how national intellectual property regimes should be best designed to benefit developing countries and how the international framework of rules might be improved and developed." This is a valuable initiative, and I hope that World Bank research can make a useful contribution to an understanding of these issues and to policy formation.

To summarize my first point: integration with the world economy is a powerful vehicle for growth and poverty reduction in developing countries, but it would be still more powerful if the rich countries opened their own economies to a greater extent. It is in the interest of developing countries to work to enhance the openness of the trade regime and to participate in the WTO. Looking forward, we should support the active participation of developing countries in setting the agenda for the next round of trade liberalization talks, to take up these issues of OECD protectionism, labor and environmental standards, and intellectual property rights. The World Bank is eager to be a partner in this endeavor, and we have oriented much of our trade research over the past several years toward providing developing countries with the data and the ideas necessary for effective involvement in the negotiations.

Complementary Institutions and Policies

My second point is that developing countries themselves can take action to ensure that they benefit more strongly from globalization, in particular by building institutions and policies that can support and complement the expansion of trade.

Opening Markets

Before turning to these complementary measures, let me first stress that a developing country's own policies on trade and investment can be damaging to integration and development. It is sometimes tempting to push for market opening in other countries while protecting domestic industries and services. Such a strategy is more likely to impede development than to promote it. Countries benefit from their own market opening in many ways. One is technological and managerial: foreign direct investment brings with it innovations in product, process, and organizational technologies, while importation of goods brings embedded technologies and access to lower-cost production inputs and consumer goods. Another benefit is greater efficiency: competition from abroad spurs domestic industry to make productivity improvements, promoting growth and employment over the medium term. It would therefore be a mistake for developing countries to cite hypocrisy in the trade policies of rich countries as an excuse to delay market opening. Liberalization, if accompanied by appropriate policy and institutional reforms, will help the liberalizing country, even though the gains would be still greater if the richer countries reduced their protection.

A Sound Investment Climate

Now let me turn to these complementary policies and institutions. Open trade and investment policies will generate little benefit if other institutions and policies are not in place. I like to sum up these other policies in the phrase "the investment climate." The investment climate is affected by a number of factors: macroeconomic stability; the degree of bureaucratic harassment, especially in the administration of regulations and taxes; the strength of financial institutions; the rule of law, including law enforcement; the incidence of corruption and crime; the quality of infrastructure, including power and telecommunications; the effectiveness of the government in providing sound regulatory structures for the private sector; the effective provision of public services or the framework for such services; and the quality of the labor force. By this last point I mean not only the level of skills but also the prevailing work culture and the state of labor relations. If you have an unreliable power supply, no financial depth, lots of harassment from government officials, a high level of corruption, and a very low skill base, then more open trade and investment policies, beneficial though they are likely to be, are unlikely to generate large increases in productive investment and employment.

Investigation of the key determinants of the investment climate and how to improve it is one of the important areas in which I am trying to expand the research agenda at the World Bank. We have been trying to better understand the investment climate by helping clients systematically survey private firms, focusing especially on small and medium-size enterprises (SMEs). It is usually these enterprises that suffer most when the investment climate is hostile. The development experience of the countries of East Asia, notably Japan and China, have shown us the great importance of SMEs in driving economic growth.

Let me share with you the results of our recent survey in India, which was done in collaboration with the industry federation. India has become much more open at the national level but is seeing mixed results at the state level because the investment climate varies so much across states. Our survey covered 10 states, and we found a clear pattern. Several states have a poor investment climate—for example, unreliable power supplies, onerous regulations, and intrusive and disruptive visits from government officials, all of which add up to higher costs. We estimate that for some states these costs are analogous to an additional tax of 20 to 30 percent. Not surprisingly, states with weak investment climates have less investment, less growth, and less poverty reduction (CII and World Bank 2001).

I think this is a key area on which the World Bank should focus: helping countries analyze and improve their investment climates so that they attract from their own citizens and from foreign investors efficient investment that produces jobs, higher incomes, and poverty reduction.

Freedom and Globalization

While I am on the subject of institutions that complement globalization, I would like to touch briefly on the issue of freedom, both economic and political. There is no doubt that economic freedom is vital to development and poverty reduction. Over the long run, societies in which individuals, households, and firms have the freedom to make key economic decisions that affect them directly have consistently outperformed those in which the government has arrogated those decisions to itself. Economies cannot succeed without reasonably well-functioning governments, and indeed, such government is vital to economic freedom. But neither can economies succeed if governments overreach in ways that undermine the incentives for and the dynamism of the private sector.

Political freedoms, and democracy more generally, can promote development in several ways. First, they serve as a bulwark protecting economic freedoms. Freedom of speech and freedom of assembly make it possible to organize against government decisions that would reduce economy-wide dynamism to benefit a minority. Second, democratic political systems have the information flows and responsiveness necessary to prevent the worst types of economic volatility from occurring; as Amartya Sen has emphasized, democracies do not experience famines (Sen 1999). Third, there is some evidence that democracies respond to and adapt more rapidly to external economic shocks, such as the one that hit East Asia in 1997, because they are able to share the costs of adjustment in a way that is perceived to be fair. In the same way, democracies may be better able to mediate the tradeoffs or conflicts that inevitably occur in development. For example, well-managed openness will raise incomes and reduce income poverty.

The effects of openness on a culture are likely to be unpredictable. Some people in a society will value the outside influence on culture positively; others may see it as negative. No economist or technician can decide whether the net benefit of openness for poverty reduction outweighs any net cost in terms of culture; only democratic participation can make that choice effectively. In my view, democratic participation is vital for managing the social and political tensions that inevitably accompany globalization.

Finally, history tells us that political freedom is highly valued as an end in itself, over and above any effect it might have on other dimensions of development.

Principles of Decentralization

Like many other countries, Indonesia is simultaneously decentralizing and globalizing. We know from our work elsewhere that decentralization, and the greater local participation it can generate, can improve accountability and the delivery of public services. In Central America and in India, as I have seen on recent visits, increased participation of parents in school management has improved student outcomes. Decentralization can also allow scope for local policy and project experimentation, which can lead to innovations that may then be imitated by other states. Here in Indonesia, the Kecamatan Development Project and the related Village Infrastructure Project have successfully empowered villagers by putting as many development decisions as possible directly into villagers' own hands, with high rates of return. There are, however, risks to decentralization. For example, irresponsible budget decisions by states and localities can add up to macroeconomic instability, and tax competition among them can lead to a "race to the bottom" that benefits no one. Finally, decentralization, if improperly managed, can exacerbate regional inequalities.

As Indonesia embarks on a rapid and radical decentralization program, these new challenges will confront leaders and institutions not only at the district level but also in the central government. A center that is, fiscally and in other respects, strong in relation to the provinces and districts is part of Indonesia's history and its institutions. Districts with delegated funds will have new responsibilities, but the center will, for the foreseeable future, retain an important responsibility for distributing these funds. This function has important implications not only for equity and the direct benefits of expenditures but also for how the central government goes about establishing an incentive framework for districts to do their best within their means. Mechanisms for transparency and accountability at the local level, although important, will not entirely replace accountability to the center. Instead, the two will develop and change jointly.

In building new institutions, it will be important to clarify responsibilities, both for taxes and for expenditures. First, it is important that the tax bases at the national and subnational levels be kept distinct. Otherwise, there will be opportunities for gaming between the two levels, which will damage incentives for revenue collection, lead to distortions, and create the potential for harassment of taxpayers. Second, the allocation of spending responsibility should be matched, as far as possible, by the ability to carry through implementation efficiently. Here, administrative capacity will be of great importance, as will be any externalities between subnational entities, including externalities of networking and coordination. The problems of making decentralization work are major, urgent, and difficult.

The Role of International Markets and Sequencing

My third theme is that international markets can be used to strengthen institutions and policies.

The importance of building complementary institutions and policies for reaping the benefits from global integration inevitably raises the question, should countries first make sure that all their institutions are strong before opening up? The answer is clearly, no.

Developing countries that have done well have taken a step-by-step approach toward liberalizing different types of exchange. Let me illustrate the importance of this with Indonesia's own experience. I think that there is broad agreement now that one factor behind Indonesia's financial crisis was the lethal combination of an open capital account, weak domestic financial institutions, and weak economic governance. We know now, and perhaps should have known before, that this combination can lead to serious problems of currency volatility and to banking crises. Russia's experience is another important example in which weak institutions combined with an open capital account to cause trouble.

We can think of this as a sequencing issue. Intelligently utilized, the international market for financial, legal, and accounting services can help develop a sound financial sector and better economic governance. Thus, the practical issue is which steps to take first, not whether to choose integration or isolation. Trade in financial services is not the same as, and indeed need not be tied to, trade in financial claims. Indonesia had restrictive policies regarding the provision by foreign financial institutions of services to domestic firms and consumers. The evidence from other countries is that participation of foreign financial institutions strengthens the financial system. What happened in Indonesia in the 1990s was that weak domestic financial institutions were allowed easy access to international capital markets. We now know that this sequencing can be disastrous.

The rapid growth of trade in services is one of the interesting developments of the past decade. These markets can be used to ensure good provision of power, telecommunications, and accounting services and even customs and tax administration, as well as financial services. By increasing the efficiency and reducing the costs of core business services, openness in these areas feeds directly into improved productivity and competitiveness for other downstream manufactures and services.

What are the implications for Indonesia? Simply put, a top priority must be to strengthen financial institutions—with the help of greater use of trade in services. Given a stronger financial sector, an open capital account can be a useful disciplinary device for economic policy. Without those improvements, capital account openness can translate once again into financial volatility and recession.

Pro-Poor Globalization

My topic today is globalization and poverty, and this theme has, at least implicitly, run through much of what I have said. But let me turn to it more directly. Do poor people really benefit from globalization?

Globalization, Income Inequality, and Poverty Reduction

One of the most common claims today is that globalization typically leads to growing income inequality within countries, so that its benefits go primarily to the rich. This claim is simply not true; in fact, it is one of the big myths of the antiglobalization movement. Certainly there are important examples, notably China, where opening has gone hand in hand with rising inequality, but that has not been a general pattern. In many developing countries—for instance, Ghana, Uganda, and Vietnam—integration with the international market has coincided with stable inequality or with declines in inequality. Furthermore, in China's case the rise in inequality had more to do with the establishment of market-oriented incentives in a previously centrally planned economy than with China's opening to international markets.

When trade liberalization is accompanied by stable or declining inequality, the benefits for the poor are quite powerful. In Vietnam the per capita income of the poor has been rising at about 5 percent per year since the country's opening-up began in the early 1990s. The share of the population in poverty (that is, living below a 2,000-calorie-per-day poverty line) was cut in half within a decade, from 75 percent in 1988 to

37 percent in 1998. In the case of Vietnam we have a particularly good data set for analyzing the effects of reform, and we have found that of the poorest 5 percent of households in 1992 (at the start of reform), an incredible 98 percent was better off six years later. Here, the link from trade to poverty reduction was very clear: Vietnam has become a major exporter of rice, and many of the poor are rice farmers. Furthermore, it has become a major exporter of garments and footwear, and the jobs created in these expanding sectors pay far more than the factory jobs available before the opening. Ghana and Uganda are other instructive examples from the low-income world; in each case the income of the poor has been rising at 3 or 4 percent per year during the reforms. The better prices that farmers get from exporting products such as cocoa and coffee is a key reason why openness has benefited many of the poor in these countries.

Even where inequality has increased, globalization has still led to rapid poverty reduction. China is perhaps the best example. But the benefits of globalization for the poor are particularly strong where inequality is stable or declining. I now turn to this important question of how to make globalization and growth pro-poor.

Making Globalization More Favorable to the Poor

While it is important to realize that, even without special measures within countries, globalization as defined above will generally benefit the poor, there is no reason why we should be satisfied with that result. Countries can take steps to make globalization and growth more pro-poor. The three most important ways to do this are through basic education, through social protection measures to deal with adjustments, and through measures to ensure that all regions of a country are connected to the global economy. This last concern is especially important in a vast, diverse country such as Indonesia.

Education. Basic education is critical to ensuring that everyone can participate in and benefit from growth and globalization. Many factors are important for development, but I like to emphasize the combination of a sound investment climate and good basic education. And they are complementary. A healthy, literate labor force will increase the amount of growth that results from a sound investment climate and will strongly increase the poverty reduction benefit from that growth. We should remember, too, that education is a goal in itself, a dimension of development, above and beyond its income-raising effect.

The World Bank has talked about education for a long time, but I would like to see a still stronger focus on it in our work. We know, of course, that the problem with education usually goes far beyond money; it concerns how the delivery of education is organized. As I mentioned earlier, this is an area where communities around the world are innovating. There are many examples of exciting new approaches, often more decentralized than under the old framework, with local control and parental involvement. By understanding and learning from these experiences, the World Bank can help with the design of innovations, with funding them, and—critically important—with the evaluation and dissemination of lessons.

Social protection. In discussing the benefits of openness I do not want to minimize the problems of adjustment. Much of the benefit of openness comes through more competitive markets. When countries open up particular markets, we often see a common pattern, of which the Indian machine tool industry, studied by Sutton (2000), provides a concrete example. When protection of the industry was reduced in the early 1990s, the first thing that happened was that Taiwanese firms came in and claimed about one-third of the Indian market. That was a boon to firms that needed high-quality machine tools, but it obviously created a tremendous problem for the large domestic machine tool industry. (Remember that a quota is a subsidy to producers of a good by the consumers of that same good.) After nearly a decade of more open policies, what has happened is that several Indian producers have adapted; they have dramatically increased productivity, introduced new products, reclaimed much of the market—and started to export. The higher productivity and better quality of product are among the sources of the gains from openness.

But during the adjustment, some workers and firm owners lost their employment and their incomes. During any liberalization process, there are going to be winners and losers, among the poor and the nonpoor alike. To help prevent people from falling into poverty, and to smooth adjustment, social protection measures, tailored to country circumstances, are essential. While unemployment insurance can be important for formal sector workers, other approaches, such as public work schemes of the food-for-work variety, are much more likely to reach the truly poor. Good social protection is not just a short-run palliative but an essential underpinning of a market economy, to make it function well and to involve poor people in the opportunities it creates. Without good social protection, poor people may be unable to take some of the risks that are part of participation in a market economy, even when they stand to gain. Governments should provide leadership in the move toward openness. Because there will always be myopic or vested interests opposed to reform, governments should encourage people to recognize the long-term benefits of openness rather than just the short-run adjustment costs. At the same time, governments need to use social protection to share and minimize the costs of adjustment.

Regional policies. A simple statement of how to realize strong benefits from globalization would be, "create a sound investment climate and provide education for all." But much of what goes into the investment climate is a local issue, such as local government regulation and the quality of local infrastructure. I used India as an example of how these factors can vary dramatically across states. States or districts with weak investment climates tend to become concentrations of poverty. A key measure, or set of measures, for ensuring that poor people benefit from globalization is to strengthen the investment climate throughout the country rather than just in the highest-capacity (often, the wealthier) states.

Conclusion

Indonesia is well down the road toward integration with the global economy. Unlike many other countries, Indonesia recognized decades ago that integration is a vital ingredient of long-term development and poverty reduction. It saw early on that overreliance on petroleum exports was not the type of integration that would lead to the fastest possible development, and it took the policy steps necessary to engage with the world by promoting manufactured exports and foreign direct investment. I would urge you not to let the severe recent difficulties shake that view or halt your momentum toward integration. The recent crises have underlined the importance of sequencing policy reforms, and especially of getting key elements of governance right. But at the same time, both the longer-term history of East Asia and its recoveries from crises have shown just how effective globalization can be in achieving development goals.

With the greater economic and political freedom that it now has, and with far-sighted leadership, Indonesia has the opportunity to make the necessary adjustments and to continue its progress. I have outlined four steps along that road: opening the economy, building the needed supporting institutions and policies, sequencing reforms appropriately, and adopting the measures needed to make globalization more pro-poor. Indonesia's past record makes me confident that it will be possible to take all these steps, with tremendous long-term results for poverty reduction. And we will join you in pressing rich countries to dismantle their protection.

Let me close by emphasizing again where I see a key role for the World Bank and for development assistance more generally: to support countries, and communities, in developing a sound investment climate and ensuring that education is provided for all. A crucial problem today is that quite a few poor countries, and poor people within countries, are simply not participating in globalization, either because the country's trade and investment policies are highly restrictive or because other important ingredients, such as infrastructure, rule of law, or education, are missing. The problem for many of the poor is not the effects of globalization but, rather, the consequences of being left out of globalization. Together, we must work to ensure that the poor can participate fully and reap the benefits of globalization.

Investing in Education and Institutions: The Path to Growth and Poverty Reduction in Pakistan

Nicholas Stern

National Workshop on Pakistan's Poverty Reduction Programme, Islamabad, March 29, 2001

I am delighted to have this opportunity to return to Pakistan. I visited this country often in the 1980s and found it to be a place of enormous possibilities. At that time, the macroeconomic aggregates suggested that Pakistan was doing well. The economy had grown strongly throughout the 1960s and 1970s, with growth rates averaging 6.8 percent in the 1960s and 4.5 percent in the 1970s. Even between 1980 and 1985, Pakistan's growth rate averaged a very respectable 6.7 percent (Figure 1), and poverty declined sharply during those years.

Since the early 1990s, however, Pakistan's growth has slowed, to just 3.7 percent a year during 1995–2000. With the population growing at a rapid 2.5 percent a year, growth in per capita income has thus dropped to slightly over 1 percent. Poverty rates, at around one-third, are back to the levels of about 20 years ago. It appears that the gains of the 1980s were canceled out in the 1990s. Other social indicators have deteriorated too. Unless these negative trends are reversed, and reversed quickly, the strains on the social fabric of the nation could become unbearable.

Recovering from the Lost Decade

In retrospect, this deceleration in growth should not be so surprising. When we look back at the period from the 1960s through the early 1980s, it is clear that growth was driven largely by external factors such

I am most thankful to Elizabeth King for her contribution to the development of this lecture. I also owe a debt of gratitude to Shahrokh Fardoust, Emmanuel Jimenez, Harold Alderman, Hope Neighbor, Andrew Mason, Halsey Rogers, William Byrd, John Panzer, and William Easterly for their contributions.

Figure 1. Growth of Gross Domestic Product (GDP), Pakistan, 1966–99

Percent

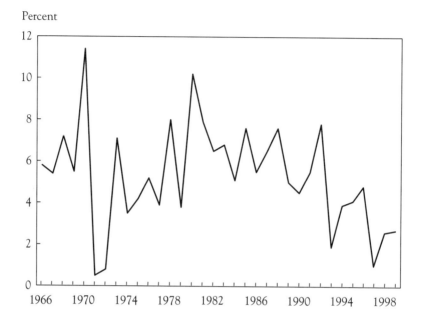

Source: World Bank WDI central database.

as flows of aid, remittances, and the technology of the Green Revolution, rather than by a strong, reforming domestic climate for growth. When the flows from abroad began to dry up in the late 1980s and early 1990s, and when the agricultural innovations had worked their way through the system, growth dropped off.

This is not to say that the deceleration was inevitable. India's experience over the same period underlines this point. Pakistan grew faster than India through the 1980s, but since the early 1990s India has grown at a significantly higher rate—about 6 percent a year, compared with 3.7 percent a year in Pakistan. What made India's rapid growth possible was a reform program that increased openness and competitiveness while improving major elements of its investment climate, both at the national level and in some states. India also took steps to increase the inclusiveness of growth by expanding education, including education of girls. As a result, its literacy rate has risen over the past decade, and the female literacy rate has increased significantly.

The negative shocks that Pakistan experienced (or, rather, the end of positive shocks) made its problems in these areas of investment climate and inclusiveness of people apparent. Yet in contrast to India, Pakistan failed to take the necessary steps to overcome those problems. The result, as the governor of the State Bank argued in Karachi earlier this year and as the finance minister said at the recent Pakistan Development Forum in Islamabad, is that the 1990s represented "a lost decade for Pakistan."

So this is a real moment of challenge. The task facing Pakistan is to turn around the past decade's disappointments in investment climate, growth, and poverty reduction. Today, I would like to talk about how Pakistan might not only return to higher levels of growth but also ensure that growth benefits the poor. I believe that Pakistan can do this, but it will require a concerted effort to improve the climate for investment and increase the inclusiveness of growth, through education and by closing the education gender gap.

In developing this argument, I will make four points:

- First, Pakistan can improve its *investment climate*; that is, it can change its institutions and policies in ways that will encourage investment and allow the country to realize higher returns from its human and physical capital.

- Second, *education* is paramount: Pakistan will achieve sustained and faster economic growth only if it succeeds in improving the quality of its labor force. Education will also increase the inclusiveness of growth.

- Third, Pakistan's greatest challenge in education is to improve the *educational levels of the poor, people in rural areas, and, especially, girls*. Reducing the gender education gap yields great payoffs, and I will discuss in detail how this might be achieved.

- Fourth, there are well-defined *reforms in education policy and institutions* that have already proved successful, abroad or within Pakistan, and that could spur innovation, improve the quality of schooling, and deepen Pakistan's human capital base.

Pakistan is a country with tremendous potential. It has shown in the past that it can grow rapidly, and it has deep reserves of capable people (some of whom, incidentally, I have had the great pleasure of serving with in academic life and at the World Bank). The key is to create a policy and institutional environment that will tap this great potential, encourage the productive use of human and physical capital, and ensure that all Pakistanis can participate in and contribute to the resulting growth. If Pakistan can do this, there is no reason why it cannot develop rapidly, as its neighbors China and India have done in the past two decades. Both countries launched ambitious reforms in difficult circumstances. Pakistan, too, can turn its current difficulties into a catalyst for change.

Strengthening Pakistan's Institutions and Policies

If Pakistan is to embark on a path of growth and poverty reduction, it is vital that it improve its investment climate. As the finance minister emphasized in his address to the Pakistan Development Forum, the revival of economic growth is an essential part of the government's own strategy for bettering the lives of its people. But growth depends on higher private investment and more productive use of capital (physical and human), which in turn are enabled by a sound investment climate. By investment climate, I mean the policy and institutional environment, both present and expected, that affects the returns and risks associated with investment.

Seen in this broad way, the investment climate clearly depends on many different aspects of public and private action. It is useful to group the elements of the investment climate into three categories:

- *Stability and openness*—macroeconomic stability, trade openness, competitive domestic markets, and political and social stability

- *Governance and institutions*—a strong legal and regulatory framework; efficient government; low levels of bureaucratic harassment and corruption, especially in the areas of regulation and taxation; effective corporate governance; strong and secure financial institutions; a high-quality labor force; good labor relations; effective provision of public services; a well-functioning, even-handed judicial system; and low levels of crime

- *Infrastructure*—a modern telecommunications system, dependable supplies of power and water, and extensive transport infrastructure

Many countries in the developing world have made great progress in increasing *stability and openness* over the past two decades. Most economies are more open: average tariff levels have declined sharply in all developing regions since the first half of the 1980s, and the dispersion of tariffs has also narrowed in many countries. Inflation rates have fallen sharply, both in level and in variability, and this development has increased macroeconomic stability and reassured domestic and foreign investors. On the political side, the number of the world's countries that are democracies has doubled over the past quarter-century, reducing possible disturbances from government transitions. There remains great room for improvement in the stability and openness category; trade restrictions, for example, could be reduced in most developing countries—and in industrial countries, too—but the extent of recent progress should be recognized and welcomed.

Greater stability and openness have contributed to more rapid development in a variety of economies, including those of Pakistan's giant neighbors. Yet far too many countries that have implemented macro reforms have failed to see the expected acceleration in investment, growth, and poverty reduction. The reasons can typically be traced to shortcomings in the other two broad elements of the investment climate: governance and institutions, and infrastructure.

Governance and institutions have a large effect on the expected productivity returns to investment; they influence how difficult or easy it is to register and start firms, to move goods in and out of the country through customs, and to pay taxes in a fair and transparent way. For example, poor governance and excessive bureaucratic harassment have been major impediments to investment and growth in Eastern Europe and Central Asia; according to our surveys, firm managers in that region must spend twice as much time with government officials as do their counterparts in Latin America.

The quality of different types of *infrastructure*—power, ports, telecommunications, roads, rail, and so on—is also a crucial part of the story. Poor infrastructure translates directly into higher costs for producers, reducing their productivity and dependability as suppliers. One example comes from detailed firm surveys carried out in India (CII and World Bank 2001). In the states with the poorest overall investment climate—which, not surprisingly, are the states with the least dependable power supplies—virtually all firms have had to invest in their own private generators. This power commitment and redundancy is very costly, especially for small and medium-size enterprises (SMEs), and it directly decreases the vitality of the SME sector.

Pakistan's Investment Climate

How does Pakistan look when we examine it through the lens of the investment climate? As I suggested earlier, the overall view is not attractive. On the macro and trade policy front, Pakistan has made some progress in stabilizing the economy and in moving to a more open trade regime. In trade policy, it has lowered its maximum tariff rate to 35 percent (to be reduced further, to 30 percent, in July 2001), and few quantitative restrictions remain. But these tariff rates are still relatively high by international standards (for example, compared with industrial countries and East Asia), and there is still too much variation in effective protection, much of it related to lobbying by import-substituting industries.

Another positive development is that the floating of the interbank exchange rate in July 2000 resulted in modest depreciation, improving price incentives for exporters. And inflation has been in the low single digits for some time.

But other elements of the macro policy mix do not look as good, such as the fiscal stabilization implemented through expenditure cutbacks (rather than through higher tax revenues from an expanded tax base) and the high real interest rates on borrowing from the financial sector. In general, the probability that current macroeconomic and trade policies will be sufficient to revive growth does not seem high. Moreover, Pakistan's agricultural production and its overall economic growth in the short run are being severely affected by the drought affecting Balochistan Province and parts of Sindh Province and by the subnormal precipitation that is reducing water availability in the Indus River system.

Aside from these problems, there is now widespread recognition that simply getting macro and trade policies right will not be sufficient; these policies will need to be supported by a complementary set of policy and institutional reforms that improve the rest of the investment climate. The consistently poor investment climate, which deteriorated further in the late 1990s, has contributed to weak economic performance and a drop in the human capital investments that are essential to sustained long-term growth for Pakistan.

The competitiveness of Pakistan's agricultural and industrial sectors has been damaged by numerous micro-level state interventions, through a complex net of protectionism, tax exemptions, guarantees, and subsidized credit and inputs. As in many other countries, such policies can be taken over by special interest groups or undermined by corruption. Businesses in Pakistan complain of pervasive harassment and bribe-taking by the numerous government agencies that regulate their activities. Not only are the services that these agencies are supposed to provide of poor quality or virtually nonexistent, but the associated corruption and harassment in themselves constitute a significant burden on the private sector and a disincentive for investment. Businessmen also complain about policy uncertainty, frequent reversals of policies, and tailor-made incentives that distort the environment in which they work and make them less willing to invest.

Although Pakistan is not the only country that has found it difficult to reform public sector institutions, it falls well below the average on key aspects of the investment climate in cross-country analyses (Figure 2), even when we consider countries with similar income levels. Recent World Bank research suggests that Pakistan fares worse than the norm, for countries of similar income, on key dimensions of governance; for example, it has less effective government and more graft. It is precisely performance on these types of indicators that will determine whether Pakistan can spur productive investment, both domestic and foreign, and capitalize on that investment.

Figure 2. Pakistan's Performance on Key Governance Indicators
(cross-country mean = 0; range is approximately –2.5 to 2.5)

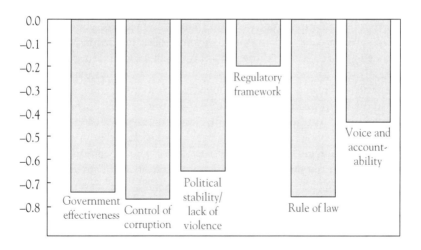

Source: Kaufmann, Kraay, and Zoido-Lobatón 1999a, 1999b.

Creating a Favorable Climate for Investment

The government is striving to foster a positive business environment for
the revival of investment and growth, this time on a sustainable basis.
Improving the investment climate through better governance has been
one of its top priorities, and progress has been made in some areas. For
example, the government has worked to rebuild its credibility by following through on its policies, avoiding reversals for the most part, re-
establishing and adhering to a stabilization program supported by the
International Monetary Fund (IMF), and agreeing on new debt resched-
uling with the Paris Club. What is perhaps most notable is that the
long-drawn-out dispute with the Hub Power Company, which to a considerable extent had poisoned the atmosphere for foreign investment,
has finally been resolved. The government is also trying to accelerate its
privatization program, especially in the banking sector, and it is establishing price and regulatory frameworks to encourage private investment
in the energy sector, particularly in gas.

These are all steps in the right direction, but turning around the investment climate will take time, and more needs to be done. The central
theme must be to reduce the unnecessary costs of doing business in
Pakistan—costs related to excessive regulation, the associated poor
governance, distortionary taxation, and the burden emanating from
inefficient public sector enterprises. It is also extremely important to
maintain a level playing field for different industries and firms rather
than provide firm- or industry-specific incentives.

Further deregulation, improved governance, and reduced corruption will
help lower the cost of doing business. Particularly important are governance improvements in those parts of the public sector that interact
directly with private businesses, including the tax and customs authorities, the police, and the army of labor, safety, environmental, and other
government inspectors. Wholesale restructuring of the Central Board of
Revenue and its transformation into a modern, taxpayer-friendly institution would make a huge difference in improving the business environment. On the regulatory front, the host of laws and regulations
impinging on the private sector needs to be rationalized, streamlined,
and simplified. This would not only ease the direct burden on the private sector of complying with regulations but would also sharply reduce
the scope for discretion, harassment, and corruption.

The government's plans for accelerated privatization should be implemented. Early successes in a few large privatization transactions—in

telecommunications, banking, or energy—would send an extremely important signal about the government's commitment and would in themselves improve the investment climate. Before pressing ahead with such transactions, the government will need first to establish credible pricing and regulatory frameworks and to complete the necessary corporate, financial, and employment restructuring.

Privatization will also help reduce the costs and improve the quality of goods and services that are now provided to the private sector by public sector enterprises. The inefficiency of the public sector transport infrastructure, including railways, ports, airlines, and roads, imposes significant costs on private sector activity and exports. Tariff protection for Pakistan's inefficient public sector steel producer means that downstream users of steel pay prices well above those prevailing on world markets. Privatization or, where privatization is not feasible, closure of the public sector producers will reduce costs to the public sector and improve the investment climate for the private sector.

Finally, some sectors have real potential for attracting large amounts of foreign direct investment fairly quickly. The most notable example is natural gas, where the exploitation of the resources discovered in recent years could improve Pakistan's balance of payments by $500 million or more per year through substitution of gas for imported oil. The government has already announced two substantial increases in the gas price and is developing a suitable regulatory and institutional framework.

Pakistan's Education Record:
Missed Opportunities for More Rapid Development

Let me turn now to a discussion of educational performance and educational reform. Education takes center stage in any discussion of development strategy, for two reasons. First, the quantity and quality of education strongly influence the labor force, governance, and the workings of most institutions. Education is thus a key determinant of the investment climate. Firms, whether domestic or foreign, are more eager to invest when they know that they will be able to draw on a skilled work force to make that investment productive. Second, universal access to basic education is essential for ensuring that all segments of society benefit from macroeconomic growth.

Studies from various parts of the world confirm that the productivity benefits of education are large: just one additional year of education can increase productivity in wage employment by 10 percent, even after controlling for other factors. Why is this relationship so strong? One reason is that a better-educated person is more flexible; she absorbs new information faster and applies unfamiliar inputs and new processes more effectively. In the uncertain and dynamic environment of rapid technical change, more highly educated workers have a big advantage. More education and skills allow people to adopt and profit from new work opportunities and new technology.

In addition, there are strong complementarities between human capital and other forms of investment. In settings where average educational levels are as low as those in Pakistan, the full returns to physical investments, whether private or public, will not be realized without concomitant investments in education. Those who are more educated are poised to benefit from the opportunities afforded them through extra capital, while those who are poorly educated (usually because of their income poverty) are not. For example, in rural Vietnam there is evidence of strong complementarities between irrigation infrastructure and primary education that affect the returns to expansion of irrigation (Van de Walle 2000) and so have a direct effect on income growth of the poor. Having a literate and healthy labor force increases the amount of growth that is enabled by physical investments—and it strongly increases the poverty reduction benefit from that growth.

Education can also be a bulwark against volatility for the poor. Even the fundamental skills learned in primary school can make a critical difference for the survival of families when government services fall short or during times of economic crisis. Education is not only a tool for raising or maintaining the incomes of the poor; it is also an end in itself. Poverty is increasingly recognized as consisting of deprivation along multiple dimensions, so that lack of education is itself a form of poverty. The widening of educational access can thus help to eradicate poverty even before it begins to yield returns in the labor market.

Education holds out the promise of greater productivity and inclusion. Has Pakistan's education system delivered on this promise? Clearly not; by international standards, Pakistan's overall performance in education has been poor. As Figure 3 shows, Pakistan's primary enrollment rates are far below those expected for its level of income. Within the South Asian region, Pakistan lags well behind its neighbors in enrollment: net primary enrollment rates are 75 percent in Bangladesh, 77 percent in India, and 100 percent in Sri Lanka, but only 50 or 51 percent in Pakistan. Because of its slowness in increasing educational levels for the bulk

Figure 3. Net Primary Enrollment in Low-Income Countries, 1997

Net primary enrollment rate

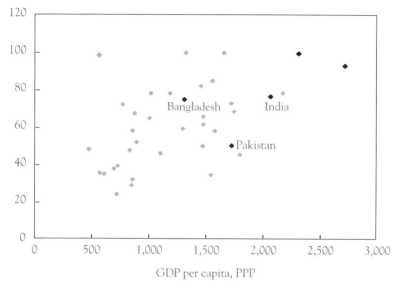

GDP per capita, PPP

Note: GDP, gross domestic product; PPP, purchasing power parity. Enrollment figure for Pakistan is for 1999. Low-income countries are those with 1999 gross national product (GNP) per capita of less than $755, World Bank's Atlas method.
Source: World Bank 1999a; Pakistan Integrated Household Survey (PIHS) 1998–99.

of its labor force, Pakistan has missed important economic opportunities that many developing countries, including its neighbors, have seized. And even though adult literacy rates in Pakistan are similar to those of its neighbors, its lower enrollment rates mean that its literacy levels will lag in the future. This will further weaken Pakistan's competitiveness in the world economy, as well as the ability of its poor to participate in the development process.

Pakistan's education system is not any better at promoting inclusion. Micro evidence shows huge discrepancies among social groups in access to education. The enrollment statistics reveal three major social divides. The first is the wide gap between school enrollment rates for children living in cities and in rural areas (Figure 4). In Sindh Province, for example, enrollment rates for urban children are nearly twice as high as those for rural children. The second, and related, gap is between

Figure 4. Urban-Rural Inequalities in Primary Education, Pakistan, Selected Provinces, 1997

Net primary enrollment rate

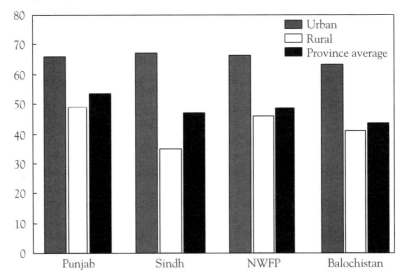

Note: NWFP, Northwest Frontier Province.
Source: PIHS 1998–99.

children from rich and poor families. The enrollment rate in primary education is only 40 percent among the poorest 10 percent of the population, or 60 percentage points lower than for the richest 10 percent, who have reached virtually universal enrollment. The size of the rich-poor gap varies across Pakistan's provinces, but everywhere the same pattern emerges: a large proportion of today's school-age children are not acquiring the fundamental knowledge and skills that would enable them to participate fully in their country's economic, social, and political development. The third major social divide in enrollment is along gender lines, and I will explore it in greater detail.

Gender and Education: The Returns from Investing in Girls

The shortcomings of Pakistan's educational performance in the aggregate can be attributed largely to its poor record in educating girls. Only in Punjab do girls' enrollment rates at the primary level approach even

50 percent, while in Balochistan only about one-third of girls who should be in primary school are enrolled (Figure 5). Although mean boys' enrollment rates are not high either, especially among the poor, overall educational levels cannot be improved without making a significant advance in the education of girls.

Ten years ago, Lawrence Summers, then the chief economist of the World Bank, spoke here on the critical importance of girls' education to Pakistan's development—indeed, to any country's development. He called education the "highest-return investment available in the developing world." Over the past decade, the evidence in favor of this proposition has become ever more detailed, wide-ranging, and powerful. At this stage of Pakistan's development, investing in female education is a critical link for Pakistan's prospects for faster growth and performance on several human development indicators.

We know from many studies that mothers' illiteracy and lack of schooling directly disadvantage their young children. Children under five are

Figure 5. Gender Inequality in Education, Pakistan, Provinces, 1997

Net primary enrollment rate

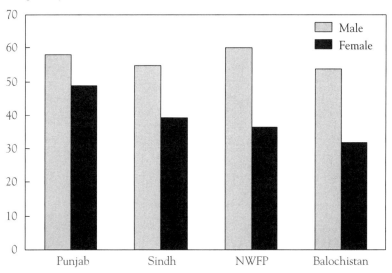

Note: NWFP, Northwest Frontier Province.
Source: PIHS 1998–99.

more likely to survive if their mothers have some primary schooling than if they have no schooling, and the probability of survival is even higher if their mothers have some secondary schooling. In fact, in Pakistan the mother's schooling is almost as important as the family's income in improving a child's nutrition (Alderman and Garcia 1994). A recent cross-country study of 63 countries concludes that gains in women's education made the single largest contribution to declines in malnutrition in 1970–95, accounting for 43 percent of the total (Smith and Haddad 2000). This is because mothers with more education are more likely to adopt appropriate health-promoting practices and are better able to mitigate adverse shocks, such as price changes, that might reduce food consumption within the family. By contrast, a mother's illiteracy deprives her of knowledge and self-confidence, weakening her ability to nurture and protect her children. Consider, too, the large social cost of the resulting missed opportunities for stimulating the development of children's mental, emotional, and motor skills—opportunities that cannot easily be retrieved.

The evidence concerning the profoundly damaging effects of low educational levels for women goes far beyond malnutrition and stunted child development. Poor education also reduces the productivity of investments and weakens governance. For example, in Indonesia gender differences in wages do not accurately reflect gender differences in the effects of schooling on productivity (particularly when there is prejudice in the labor market) and so do not encourage appropriate investments in human capital. Yet educating women pays off: despite their lower wages, women, on average, receive wage increments for every additional year of schooling that are higher than those that accrue to men for every additional year of schooling (Behrman and Deolalikar 1995). At the secondary level the impact of education on women's wages is 50 percent larger than that on men's. A large number of studies of other countries echo this finding for Indonesia (Schultz 1993, 1998). In agriculture, raising the educational and input levels of female farmers relative to those of male farmers could increase total farm yields significantly (Quisumbing 1996); often, educating women has a greater marginal impact than does educating men.

The benefits of schooling are reflected also in cross-country comparisons, which show that raising women's schooling levels and narrowing the education gap between women and men contribute to higher growth. For example, one study estimated how much faster the countries of South Asia could have grown had they started with the same gender gap in schooling as prevailed in East Asia in 1960 and had they closed that gender gap as fast as East Asia did between 1960 and 1992. The study found that annual growth in income per capita could have been nearly a percentage point higher—a substantial increase over actual growth rates (Klasen 1999). Another study, after controlling for male secondary education and other variables commonly related to growth, estimated that even in middle- and high-income countries with higher initial educational levels, an increase of 1 percentage point in the share of women with secondary education was associated with a 0.3 percentage point increase in per capita income (Dollar and Gatti 1999).

I also want to mention another benefit of women's schooling levels, one that takes me back to my earlier point about the importance of the quality of governance and institutions to a country's climate for investment and growth. Raising women's schooling levels empowers women, allowing them to participate more broadly and more effectively not only in the economy as a whole but also in policymaking and government. As Figure 6 shows, this participation has positive effects on a country's prospects for development.

Figure 6. Gender Inequality and Corruption

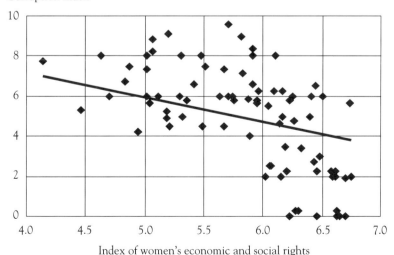

Source: World Bank 2001a; Kaufmann, 1998.

A few recent studies are beginning to document this. They conclude that governments and businesses are cleaner when women are more active in politics or business (Dollar, Fisman, and Gatti forthcoming; Swamy and others 2000). Countries with more women in parliament typically have lower levels of corruption. Swamy and others (2000), using the International Country Risk Guide's Corruption Index and Transparency International's Corruption Perceptions Index, found that a 1 standard deviation increase in the proportion of women in lower houses of parliament (from the worldwide average of 11 percent) is accompanied by no less than a 10 percent decrease in corruption. This was the case after controlling for national income and other factors shown to affect corruption, such as the extent of civil liberties and the degree of trade openness. The findings suggest that women are an effective force both for good government and for business trust. But if women's participation in political decisionmaking is to increase, they need to be literate, meaning that more girls need to go to school and stay in school longer.

Improving Education Policies and Institutions

It is clear, then, that improvements in performance in Pakistan, particularly for girls and women, could yield great potential returns in terms of development in the educational arena. But do we know how to achieve these improvements? I will argue that there is much that we have learned about the answer to this "how" question. Of course, the actual policy and institutional reforms that are designed and implemented will be a matter for Pakistan to decide, but I will set out here a menu of options that might be considered—a sampling of initiatives that have succeeded in improving the performance of education systems. Many of these models could be effective here; indeed, some of them come from within Pakistan.

While there is no single universally applicable solution, there is a general lesson to be drawn from international experience: like macroeconomic reform, effective and sustained educational reform hinges on a combination of policy and institutional changes. Investing the right amounts for the appropriate types of education is important, but it must be accompanied by an understanding of the institutional context. Governance issues affecting the delivery of education are central to effective action. We know, for example, that when the quality of the education available improves and students learn, families respond positively by sending their children to school and supporting them in their learning.

And we also know that quality improves at a school when the local community participates more actively in the school's functioning.

Pakistan has had some recent successes that point to opportunities while also serving as a warning of how such opportunities may be squandered. Let me speak first about the successes. In a five-year period from 1992 to 1997, the number of girls enrolled in primary school in Balochistan doubled, thanks to a combination of innovative programs. In rural areas of the province, the program encouraged parents to get involved in establishing schools and subsidized the recruitment of female teachers from the local community (Kim, Alderman, and Orazem 1998). In Quetta, neighborhoods were invited to open private schools that would receive support on the basis of girls' enrollment in the schools. This urban program increased girls' enrollment by one-third (Kim, Alderman, and Orazem 1999). And the drive to increase girls' education led to higher enrollment of boys—even though no subsidy was linked to boys' enrollment.

What made these programs work? What can we learn from them and from successful programs in other countries? Some lessons are summarized here.

1. If programs are designed appropriately—that is, if they take into account the traditions, cultural values, and economic conditions of families and communities that influence demand for schooling—they can succeed in drawing girls to school. In the early 1990s several surveys in Pakistan found that parents refused to send their daughters to school because the schools were too far away, there were not enough female teachers, and the schools were coeducational (Summers 1992). In recent years a nationwide scholarship program for rural girls in Bangladesh, which had similar problems, has been credited with raising girls' secondary education enrollment rates to levels approaching those of boys—a remarkable achievement. Besides building school facilities that ensure privacy for girls, hiring more female teachers, and funding tuition costs for girls, the program provides for bank accounts to be opened in the girls' names. Monthly stipends are deposited into these accounts. The stipends are not large, but they allow the girls to purchase the school and personal supplies they need to attend school—and the stipend sends a clear signal to the families about the importance of the girls' education. The program has been funded by various donor agencies, among them the World Bank, but its roots are local; it was started in the early 1980s in two communities on the initiative of a local leader. It is a tremendous example of how local

communities and nongovernmental organizations (NGOs) can help overcome culture-based obstacles to the success of public services such as education.

2. As the program in Balochistan described above demonstrates, even poor communities with a low average level of education among adults can organize around the provision of education for their children and improve school performance. Experiences elsewhere confirm this lesson. For example, El Salvador's Community-Managed Schools Program has been expanding education in rural areas by enlisting and financing community management teams to operate schools. The teams, made up of parents and elected by the community, are responsible for hiring and firing teachers and for equipping and maintaining schools, and they have the power to go with the responsibility. Experience with this program demonstrates that community-based incentives can encourage teachers to perform better (Jimenez and Sawada 1999). The program schools have lower teacher and student absenteeism than do traditional schools because the local community is involved in monitoring schools. Similar effects have been observed in India's District Primary Education Programme (also supported by the World Bank but conceived within India), in which there is strong community involvement and indirect incentives for girls' enrollment.

3. As the Balochistan program also shows, there is scope for the public and private sectors to collaborate in education, targeting low-income households. Opening up the system to nonpublic provision with public-sector financial support can increase access and improve equity. This support may go to schools themselves, as in Balochistan, or to individuals, as in the case of the bursary and voucher programs in Chile and Colombia (King, Orazem, and Wohlgemuth 1999).

There is little question that such support will increase enrollment, but will low-income families benefit? The answer from experience is that with proper attention to the design of the program, poor people can indeed be the principal beneficiaries. The Colombia program, for example, uses, in screening for participation, both the income of beneficiaries and the tuition charged by the school.

Even in Pakistan, private schools for low-income households are emerging. Two-thirds of all primary school students in low-income neighborhoods in Lahore attend private schools. This high market share of private schools is made possible in part by their low costs, tuition at many of those schools is not appreciably higher than fees and other school costs in government schools, partly because their teacher salaries are lower than in government schools. But the demand for private schools also reflects parental response to the quality of teaching. Although private schools cater to children from low-income families, on average their students score higher in language and math tests than do students in government schools, after controlling for parents' education and income (Alderman, Orazem, and Paterno 2001). So far, the expansion of private education among low-income households is largely an urban phenomenon, and most of Pakistan's poor in rural areas have not yet benefited. But the evidence from the cities will encourage rural residents, as well, to take up such opportunities as they become available.

4. Improving accountability in the civil service can help the education system function better. In most countries, the bulk of the civil service is in the education sector. When governance of public servants fails, the consequences are worst for education.

Most of you are well aware of the failure in Pakistan to provide the right incentives for the right people to become teachers and head teachers and for them to do their jobs properly once appointed. A recent study in rural areas showed that out of 125 schools visited by the survey team, only 96 were open at the time of the visit. Moreover, of these 96 schools, only half were classified as fully functional, and in almost a quarter, fewer than half of the teachers were present (Gazdar 2000). A government school teacher with one year of experience can legally miss 18 percent of the school term, and teachers also take many unauthorized leaves. In Lahore more than 40 percent of the head teachers in government schools believe that absenteeism among teachers is a serious problem, compared with 23 percent of head teachers in private schools, and there are corresponding effects on student test results (World Bank 1996).

Teacher absenteeism is only one example of how weak governance threatens the quality of education throughout Pakistan, but it is a very important one. When teachers show up in the classroom, students do too, with salutary effects on their learning. When learning increases, we see more students continuing in school and completing more years of education. These effects are larger for girls than for boys because the demand for girls' education is more responsive to whether learning actually takes place (King, Orazem, and Paterno 1999).

What are the most effective instruments for increasing accountability? Because so many other countries are grappling with the same problem, we can draw on extensive experience from both inside and outside

Pakistan for answers. What we are learning is that a well-functioning education system relies on a combination of social pressure, institutional pressure, and properly structured pay systems. I have already mentioned the important role that community monitoring can play through local school committees where local inspectorates are weak, as in the examples from Balochistan and El Salvador. When parents are involved in their local schools and have some say over how it operates, the resulting pressure can help ensure that schools are open for the expected number of school days, that students receive their textbooks, and that teachers come to school.

At the same time, it is important to improve official supervision of schools and link it to an effective system for rewarding good performance—one that underlines the importance of getting results. In Pakistan such a system is clearly lacking in the public schools. Although public school teachers receive twice the pay of private school teachers, their performance is worse, and they are absent for more than twice as many days as their counterparts in private schools. We must ask ourselves whether this behavior is likely to change as long as pay levels have very little to do with performance and there are no clear penalties for missing work. This is not to say that pay should be the only motivator: teaching is a calling, and teachers are most effective when they are motivated in part by a culture of professionalism and a desire to help students learn. Nevertheless, the design of pay systems should reinforce rather than undermine professionalism.

5. Finally, implementing reforms to improve educational outcomes in Pakistan would require a strong commitment from leaders as agents of change. Even in much richer countries that already invest heavily in education, such as the United States, the United Kingdom, and Singapore, political leaders still count improvements in education among their highest-priority issues. This message from the highest level of leadership sends an unequivocal signal to government officials and to families about the centrality of educational outcomes to the country's future.

At the working level of the education system, Pakistan has true leaders and innovators with ideas and energy. These leaders deserve strong support from above. A promotion system in which seniority is the dominant criteria—and this seems to be the case in Pakistan at all levels of education—stifles creativity and performance.

Appointments based on political connections can undermine the success of the system. Recall the interesting example in Balochistan that I cited earlier. That program was an important innovation—but for all the steps forward it represented, weak governance and corrupt leadership have resulted in a giant step backward. Donor support (including the Bank's) evaporated when there emerged a pattern of hiring unqualified teachers—sometimes even illiterate ones who had not passed the requisite exams. Subsequently, funding had to be terminated under allegations of kickbacks and unauthorized emphasis on construction. With the demise of this short-lived program, the encouraging growth in enrollments of both boys and girls that had taken place between 1992 and 1997 was arrested.

Beyond giving support to reforming and innovative leaders within the system, it is important to give them enough time to implement real reforms. In Pakistan education secretaries change frequently; in the seven years prior to May 2000, the average tenure of education secretaries was 8 months at the federal level, 9 months in Sindh, 10 months in the Northwest Frontier Province and AJK, 6 months in Balochistan, and 13 months in Punjab. One might draw the inference that as soon as a reform program begins to take shape—which almost inevitably threatens the interests of some entrenched and powerful group—the secretary is dismissed and the reform once again loses momentum.

Conclusion: Good Things Can Happen

I want to end on a note of optimism. Pakistan achieved rapid growth before 1990. It has great potential and talented entrepreneurs, and its farmers innovated strongly during the Green Revolution. It has been moving in the right direction in several areas: it is improving governance, it is working out a strategy to improve social service delivery, and it is maintaining an encouraging degree of macroeconomic stability.

Progress has been slowest in the area of reviving investment and growth. To accelerate progress, it will be important for Pakistan to maintain an appropriate macroeconomic policy mix. Elements in such a mix are likely to include:

- A tight fiscal policy based on a higher tax-to-GDP ratio (resulting from expansion of the tax base and better collection, as opposed to higher tax rates)

- Higher and more effective public expenditures, in line with achievements on the resource mobilization front

- A prudent monetary policy that avoids excessively high real interest rates which could choke off recovery of investment

- An active exchange-rate policy, to encourage exports.

As discussed earlier, however, other policy and institutional reforms will be needed to improve the investment climate. Further deregulation; accelerated privatization (with some early successes); improved governance, especially in tax administration; and efforts to attract foreign investment into key sectors with high potential, such as natural gas, will be critical elements in improving the investment climate.

On the education front, while the current situation is unsatisfactory and the road ahead is difficult, we have seen the emergence of promising policy and institutional reform options that have made a difference within Pakistan, as they have in a variety of other countries. These initiatives have involved local communities, parents, and nongovernmental agencies, working together with government financing to fill large gaps in the provision of schooling, especially for the poor, for girls, and for rural youths. For disenfranchised and vulnerable groups, local initiatives can yield far-reaching results. Such initiatives have several advantages: they build on the motivation and direct knowledge of parents and communities to enforce more effectively the implicit contract with teachers, reduce teacher absenteeism, and increase effort; they lead to program design facilities that address the social and cultural concerns of vulnerable groups; and they help to mobilize local resources.

If Pakistan were to succeed in improving overall educational levels, what would be the effect on its growth? The growth estimates reviewed in this paper suggest that if gender gaps in Pakistan could be closed at a rate comparable to what was achieved in East Asian countries, annual growth rates could be around 1 percentage point higher for an extended period.

This effect on growth is, of course, only part of the story. Improving educational outcomes would reduce other threats to human development, such as malnutrition, disease prevalence, and infant and child mortality. And there is growing evidence that educating girls improves the quality of governance and thus promotes further investments, encouraging a virtuous circle of better governance, an improved investment climate, higher growth, and lower poverty.

Pakistan cannot afford another decade of opportunities forgone because of a poor investment climate, poor educational outcomes, and large gender gaps. We know more than ever about the governance and institutional bases of growth, about the value of education and gender inclusion for economic growth and poverty reduction, and about how these forces interact. Progress on the social agenda of improving public service delivery and empowering the poor and women to participate can make a great contribution to growth. In a similar way, outcomes in the structural agenda, aimed at improving the investment climate, are vital for poverty reduction. I am certain that this country can move forward strongly on both fronts, and if this happens, I believe that Pakistan could enter a long period of very rapid growth and development.

Reform, Poverty Reduction, and the New Agenda in China

Nicholas Stern

Beijing and Qinghua Universities, Beijing, China, June 2001

It is a great pleasure for me to be able to speak to you today. Having spent six of the most fascinating months of my life teaching in Beijing in 1988, I always enjoy returning to the vibrant environment of an elite Chinese university. In those months in China, I found that students combined technical skill, a thirst for learning, radical questioning, and an extraordinary capacity for hard work—an irresistible combination for a teacher like me.

My topic today is growth and poverty reduction. I will review briefly China's remarkable past growth and then focus in greater detail on the poverty picture—both the past achievements and the remaining problems. Poverty in a world of plenty is the outstanding challenge of our time. What better place to come to discuss poverty and to learn about how to overcome it than China, which in recent years has established a record of growth and poverty reduction that is unparalleled both across nations and in the last few centuries of China's history? Finally, I will lay out what we see as the greatest remaining challenges facing China and will suggest an agenda for further reforms that can preserve the momentum of growth and poverty reduction.

Growth and Poverty Reduction in Post-reform China

A Record of Success

In terms of the number of people escaping absolute income poverty, China has undoubtedly made the largest single contribution to global

This chapter combines speeches delivered at Beijing University and Qinghua University in June 2001. I would like to thank Deepak Bhattasali, Shaohua Chen, Robert Crooks, David Dollar, Mark Dorfman, David Ellerman, Athar Hussain, Peter Lanjouw, Tamar Manuelyan Atinc, Alan Piazza, Martin Ravallion, Halsey Rogers, and Juergen Voegele for their contributions and comments. It draws on joint work with Athar Hussain and Joseph Stiglitz (see Hussain, Stern, and Stiglitz 2000).

poverty reduction of any country in the past 20 years. Using official income poverty lines as a benchmark, the number of poor in rural China fell from 250 million in 1978, the first year of the economic reforms, to around 34 million in 1999.[1] About half of this gain came between 1978 and 1985 (Figure 1). These gains are impressive not only in themselves but also in comparison with trends in much of the rest of the world. In fact, our best estimate is that while the number of poor people worldwide fell by 8 million between 1987 and 1998, the number of poor *outside China* actually increased by 82 million.

The locomotive pulling all these people out of poverty has, of course, been China's two decades of extremely rapid income growth. The market-oriented reforms launched in 1979 dramatically improved the dynamism of both the rural and urban economies. Calculations carried out by the World Bank a few years ago showed that if China's provinces were treated as separate countries—not an unreasonable notion, given their size—the 20 fastest-growing countries in the world between 1978 and 1995 would all have been Chinese.[2] This widely shared growth has dramatically reduced poverty.

In examining China's remarkable experience, some have observed that had it been possible to hold inequality constant while still achieving these growth rates, poverty reduction would have been even more rapid. This, however, is not a sensible hypothetical case. Given the starting point of a centrally planned economy, few individual incentives, and a very equal income distribution, greater income inequality was not only inevitable but also desirable in the reform process, as it helped to provide the economic incentives necessary for much of the growth that has happened in the past 20 years. Nevertheless, it is useful to understand how this inequality emerged, as it is basic to understanding the process of growth. This has been a continuous but sometimes uneven process, and it is analytically useful to split it into phases, as follows:

- *From 1978 through the mid-1980s* growth took place largely in the rural sector. The Household Responsibility System improved productivity, and prices for agricultural products remained high. Inequality

---

1. To be more precise, the official poverty line used in China in recent years is a hybrid income-consumption line and is roughly 30 percent below the standard $1 per day used generally by the World Bank and at most points in this book.

2. Note that the calculation does not bring in comparably disaggregated estimates for India, another large country with country-size provinces (in India, states) that also grew rapidly over much of this period.

Figure 1. Number of Absolute Poor in Rural China, 1978–99

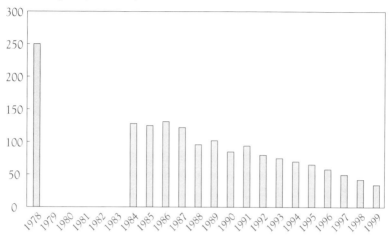

Number of poor (in million)

Source: National Bureau of Statistics (2000).

fell between urban and rural areas as the latter began to catch up with the former.

- *From the mid-1980s to the mid 1990s* rapid growth was spurred by growth in township and village enterprises (TVEs). This growth had special benefits in the intersection between rural and urban areas, as rural labor shifted toward the nonfarm economy. Public spending, including tax treatment, favored coastal areas during this period, and those areas grew rapidly. Meanwhile, the more remote areas experienced continuing lags in growth.

- *During the mid-1990s* the rural sector again enjoyed a growth surge driven by improved terms of trade for agriculture as grain procurement prices rose (that is, came closer to market levels). As a result, rural poverty fell more rapidly than it had in the previous period.

- *From the mid-1990s to today* China has returned to a growth path characterized by greater dynamism in the urban sector and in the coastal regions than elsewhere. Overall poverty reduction continues, but the most remote areas and the poorest population groups are not enjoying commensurate improvements in their living standards.

Beyond income, the reform period has also apparently seen substantial improvements in indicators of human development. Official estimates of the adult illiteracy rate have fallen by more than half, from 37 percent in 1978 to less than 17 percent in 1999. On the health front, infant and child mortality rates have also fallen, although less dramatically; the infant mortality rate fell from 41 per 1,000 live births in 1978 to 30 in 1999. These statistics are only suggestive, and they deserve further attention as better data become available. (Indeed, I hope to be able to say more on my next visit to China.)

This, then, is the backdrop against which to consider the poverty challenges facing China today: a record of great success, but with unevenness in its sectoral and geographic distribution. We must recognize, however, that this unevenness has been an inherent part of a dynamic and poverty-reducing process.

Elements of China's Success

The Chinese economy presents a mixture of features of a market economy intertwined with those of a command economy. Three institutional elements were key in the last 20 years of reforms: decentralization, rural reforms, and experimentation and innovation involving new enterprises such as TVEs. Each element is crucial to an understanding of how China was able to use its social and organizational capital to transform the economy and generate growth.

Decentralization, in its many facets, allowed experimentation and innovation without massive dislocation. The large rural sector also saw fundamental decentralization. That sector contributed productivity growth in the early stages of China's transition and served as a source of labor for industrial growth over the whole period. In turn, decentralization and rural institutions and traditions provided the basis for the new, largely collective, rural and industrial enterprises that drove China's growth beginning in the mid-1980s.

The analysis of decentralization, the rural economy, and new enterprises provides a context and rationale for China's successful evolutionary approach to the transition, which may be summarized in a stylized way in terms of four principles or observations.

- *Build on existing institutions*. The Chinese experience shows that an adaptive process of transition, proceeding step by step, can retain the social and organizational capital developed in previous stages of development and transform it in ways that enhance efficiency and productivity. Sometimes the step-by-step or incremental approach is misunderstood as being "gradual" or slow. Yet the agricultural reforms of 1978–84 probably represent the largest successful social and economic change over such a short time period ever seen in history. The reforms grew out of bottom-up experiments that were based on people's living memories of family farming. They spread horizontally in a process of social learning and then were scaled up and taken country-wide by the government. By contrast, the Russian attempt to "legislate," almost instantaneously, a large array of institutions for a market economy (of which the population had no living memory) may well take much longer to reach the goal of a well-functioning market economy. The processes employed in Russia led to the further deterioration of the country's already frail social capital, social behavior, and institutional structures and weakened incentives for innovation, investment, and structural change.

- *Adopt a learning model.* There were strong arguments in favor of following an evolutionary approach—arguments based on information, behavior, and understanding. At the outset of a reform process, it is not possible to foresee, let alone to resolve, all the problems that will emerge at later stages. Thus, change must be a process of adaptive learning, not one of following a fixed blueprint. The French have an expression for this: one learns *chemin faisant*—that is, as one goes. In the June 13, 1987, *People's Daily*, Deng Xiaoping was quoted as saying:

  Generally speaking, our rural reforms have proceeded very fast, and farmers have been enthusiastic. What took us completely by surprise was the development of township and rural industries. All sorts of small enterprises boomed in the countryside, as if a strange army had appeared suddenly from nowhere. This is not the achievement of our central government. Every year, township and village enterprises achieve 20 percent growth. This was not something I had thought about. Nor had the other comrades. It surprised us. (Quoted in Becker 2000: 68)

  China has successfully allowed regions to experiment and then has scaled up the most successful experiments to the national level.

- *Recognize the nonlinearities of reform and change.* The reform path may be more zigzag than linear, and China has in the past shown a recognition that changing circumstances require shifts in approach. To take a current example, the financial sector was quite permissive in the early stage of reform, as energies were released in the agricultural and TVE sectors, but it will now need to adapt to the basic rules of the market economy as the choices among firms and projects become more complex and the viability of the financial system comes under threat. State-owned enterprises (SOEs) have in the past played an important social welfare role for workers, but the firm-based safety net now hinders the flexibility of the labor market and dampens growth. And while decentralization of the power of taxation has had some benefits in encouraging energetic localities, it can now lead to chaotic underfunding and harassment by tax authorities.

- *Maintain social cohesion.* Change can impose strains on a society, and it is important to maintain a level of social cohesion that allows people to continue to act together. I have been impressed by China's ability to achieve collective action throughout the reform period in a variety of settings, including the TVEs and rural development initiatives. For example, on my recent visit to Shanxi Province I was struck by the ability of rural women to act together effectively in a micro-entrepreneurship effort financed by microcredit and by farmers and officials to work together on the collective organization of terracing.

As China moves forward along its reform path, it will be important to remember and maintain these broad principles. The failed reforms in many other transition economies were based on false hopes of finding shortcuts that would produce institutional reforms almost overnight (voucher privatization being one example). China has avoided the temptation to grasp at panaceas, and the same inclination will serve it well in dealing with the current challenges. New solutions will have to be found, but in the search for those new solutions it is important not to abandon the basic principles that have proved so successful up to now. Restructuring and privatization take time and care, and it is important to get them right. But this should not be cause for hesitation: precisely because the reforms do take time, there are good reasons to get on with them as soon as possible.

The Poverty That Remains

Despite the great successes of the past 20 years, there remains considerable poverty in China. I would like to return to the statistics on income poverty cited above. As a preface, let me take a moment to explain how income poverty lines are calculated so that we can understand the differences among the various lines that can be used.

Often, a statistical agency starts by calculating the cost of a minimally acceptable food basket for a household of a given size—a family of four people, say.[3] It then calculates the typical share of food in household budgets and uses that relationship to scale up the food budget to a minimum total consumption cost for the household. The final step is to use the average share of consumption in income to scale up to an income poverty line.

Using this methodology, the official income poverty line for China has been set at about $0.70 per day (calculated at 1993 PPP, or international, prices).[4] This is quite a low poverty line by world standards. If we take the more commonly used international standard for absolute poverty—$1 per day—we find that the number of income poor in China in 1999 rises to 98 million, compared with the official figure for that year of 34 million (or of 35 million–40 million, using a more comparable method of estimation based on incomes). This difference also illustrates that a large segment of the population—around 60 million people— lives from zero to 30 U.S. cents per day above the official line.

The extent of the challenge may be even greater than these figures suggest. Consumption is often a more useful gauge of a household's standard of living than income. Around China's poverty line, consumption is less than income, so the measured problem of absolute poverty is much higher when we use this metric. In 1999, 240 million people in China lived in families with consumption per person of less than $1 per day.

Combating this remaining poverty requires a good understanding of just who the remaining poor people are, where they live, and how economic developments and government programs affect them. Just what do we know about the remaining poor people? Consider the following key elements of China's poverty profile.

Individual and household characteristics of poor people. Analyses of poverty in other countries have found certain regularities in the characteristics of the individuals who make up poor households. Although we do not have access to detailed household data for China, other types of evidence suggest that similar patterns hold here.

---

3. "Minimally acceptable" can be defined in various ways, but in poor countries it is often based on key nutrients, starting with calories.

4. PPP refers to purchasing power parity. PPP estimates, which draw on international surveys of the prices of carefully specified goods, are an attempt to allow meaningful cross-country income comparisons by adjusting for differences among countries in the cost of living.

- Worldwide, *ethnic minorities* are much more likely to be poor. In China such minorities make up less than 9 percent of the total population but an estimated 40 percent of the remaining absolute poor (World Bank 2001a: 9). This preponderance of minorities among the poor is reflected in the country's poverty targeting: minority autonomous counties account for more than 40 percent of nationally designated poor counties. Much of this poverty, as we will discuss below, may be associated with geographic issues.

- *Less educated households* are highly overrepresented among the poor. Even aggregated to the provincial level, the differences between rich and poor in China are very large on this dimension: average years of schooling range from 3.5 years in the poorest provinces to about 8 years in the wealthiest (Chen and Wang 2001).

- *Female-headed households*, in many countries, are more likely to be poor than other households. Whether this is the case in China depends on the makeup of those households. If they consist primarily of households that include no able-bodied adult males, then, given the disadvantages that women face in the labor market, those households are more likely to be poor. If, instead, female-headed households in rural areas are those with an adult male who has gone to work in the city and is sending remittances back, such households may be better off than average. The little available evidence from China suggests that women do not suffer from poverty at much higher rates than do men, implying that the first story does not predominate (World Bank 2001a: 8).

- *Disability* is strongly correlated with poverty. In China analysis of the available evidence suggests that disabled people represent a large and rising share of the poor. One estimate finds that of 60 million disabled people in 1997, 17 million counted as absolute poor and 12 million were among the rural absolute poor—meaning that the disabled are far more likely to be poor than the population as a whole.[5]

Careful research based on good data is crucial for understanding the characteristics and situation of those living in poverty. China is blessed with high-quality basic data in many respects, but there remains considerable room for further improving the data and the quantity and quality of the research based on that data, as I will discuss later.

---

5. World Bank (2001a): 10, citing statistics from the China Disabled People's Federation.

Sectoral and geographic characteristics of the poor. Whether a household is poor depends not only on who lives in the household but also on where the household is located. This is true in all countries: in developing countries, for example, rural areas are generally poorer than urban areas,and this disparity is one of the drivers of rural-to-urban migration. But in China, more than in most countries, spatial discrepancies have the potential to be long-lasting. This is because the registration system and the lack of a well-developed housing market have sharply restricted worker mobility (even beyond the natural barriers to mobility found in most countries), thus weakening the natural equilibrating force of labor migration. Partly as a result, several major types of spatial disparities have emerged:

- *Urban-rural.* China has enormous urban-rural disparities in income and poverty levels—vastly greater than those in India, for example. While 27 percent of the rural population had total consumption of less than $1 per day in 1999, this was true of only 0.5 percent of the (registered) urban population.[6] Even allowing for a cost of living that is 25 percent higher in urban areas than in rural areas, the proportion of urban residents living below $1 per day rises only to 1 percent.

- *Coastal versus western provinces.* Within rural areas there are large differences in the incidence of poverty between and within provinces but most notably between the coastal provinces and the western provinces. Figure 2 illustrates the variation in provincial poverty.

- *Mountain counties and other poor counties.* About 30 percent of all counties in China are nationally designated poor counties, and others are designated "relatively poor" counties within provinces. About half of China's poor people live in these designated poor counties—53 percent in 1999 (World Bank 2001a). Many of these counties are in mountainous areas, where the challenge of integrating with the national and international economies is especially great.

The New Agenda for Reform

As is evident, even given the tremendous growth and poverty reduction of the past two decades, there is much more to be done. The key challenges that remain can be grouped into three categories:

---

6. I will return later to the problem of obtaining data on the unregistered population of rural migrants living in urban areas.

- *Deepening the private sector* by building the institutions needed to promote competitiveness, increase productivity, and create job opportunities

- *Increasing internal integration* of the economy to help attack directly the pockets of poverty that remain

- *Promoting external integration* through implementation of World Trade Organization (WTO) commitments and through assumption of a greater international role.

Since you have heard a great deal about the WTO recently, I will focus primarily on the first two challenges. Please do not misunderstand me in my choice of topics, however. China's entry into the WTO is of great importance not just for China but for the entire world.

Deepening the Private Sector

The primary challenge involved in deepening the private sector is to increase *competitiveness*. Some of the earliest sources of productivity growth, such as those arising simply from relaxing the constraints of the command economy, had big initial effects but on some dimension may be running out of steam.

The second broad challenge is *job creation*. Estimates vary considerably, but during this decade well over 100 million new jobs will have to be generated to employ workers no longer needed in agriculture, those being shed from the SOEs and TVEs, and those newly entering the work force. This sort of job creation can come only from a wider opening of the market economy both internally and externally, not through the further bloating of public sector employment.

Both increased productivity and job growth will depend on major re-forms in the financial sector, business services, and infrastructure (e.g., telecommunications and power). Institutions that are supportive in one phase of reform may, if unchanged, become fetters in the next. The new reform agenda requires a metamorphosis of existing institutions. The financial and social functions of enterprises and banks need to be sepa-rated so that China will eventually have:

- Banks that make loans for business purposes. (They cannot continue to support the social burden of the SOEs and still remain viable as banks.)

- Enterprises that operate flexibly on a market basis (not as all-inclusive, rigid providers of local public goods), with social expenditures "out in the open" and on budget, and with housing, schooling, and medical care decoupled from enterprises to improve labor mobility.

- A social security system that is publicly run and is separated from enterprises so that enterprises can be restructured and the population is provided with an adequate level of protection. This will also allow individuals to be entrepreneurial in this choice of activity and occupation.

All this is a major challenge, but it is made easier by the successes of the past 20 years. There is now a new economy out there that can both provide opportunities to draw in factors and provide a basis for taxation.

Enterprises, Competition, and the Investment Climate

A major element in deepening the private sector involves ensuring that there is vibrant competition and that this competition extends to the upstream sectors that provide financial and business services. Small firms and start-ups will play an important role in this process. Making entry and exit of firms easier is crucial to competition.

Entry: SMEs as the propeller of new growth and job creation. Economic vitality must come primarily from within—from improving the domestic investment climate so as to release more and more of the creative and entrepreneurial energies of the Chinese people.[7] Why are there still so many regulations and restrictions on the entry of new formal businesses? One reason is that governments at the national, provincial, city, and local levels want to act like good parents, always trying to protect the "children" from any possibility of getting hurt. New businesses have to pass all sorts of tests and jump over all sorts of hurdles. Sometimes these hurdles become major sources of corruption. Rather than treat the small business sector as a nursery for a few well-favored babies or milk cows for local officials, the government might do better to treat it as a spawning ground for millions of fish, with the recognition that only some will thrive.

---

7. I discussed additional aspects of investment climate in my speech "A Strategy for Development," given at the People's University of China in Beijing during this same visit to China.

What would this approach imply for the role of the government? Government interventions would need to aim at being enabling rather than restrictive or paternalistic. For example, the government might focus on reforming banks so that they can make small business loans or on eliminating restrictions on movement so that workers can go where jobs agglomerate. Enterprises and the structure of industry are elements in the provision of opportunities and in productivity growth. Competitive markets can drive that productivity growth, but they also drive structural adjustments in troubled firms. This may at first seem callous—but it is people's standard of living that matters, not the survival of specific firms. That is why some elements of social protection are not just "social programs" but key economic components in a vigorous market economy. In short, we would say: "*Protect people, not firms.*"

The reform efforts in Eastern Europe have provided many negative lessons—such as avoiding attempts to build institutions from scratch overnight—but there have also been some positive ones. One of the key lessons has been the vitality and overall success of the small and medium-size enterprise (SME) sector in countries such as Hungary and Poland.

I have already emphasized the importance of removing bureaucratic restrictions so that new small businesses can emerge and flourish. It is important to recall, however, that SMEs come not only from below (start-ups) but also from above. Reform of state-owned enterprises is a source of both medium-size firms (spin-offs or break-ups) and small businesses. The medium-size firms would be major product lines or components of the original SOE. The small businesses spawned by an SOE could originate in any aspect of the enterprise that could be handled contractually by a small business. For instance, trucks or vans could be sold over time to their drivers, creating small transport businesses that would not only serve the original firm but could also take on other business and other workers.[8] Similarly, the vehicle repair shop in the big firm could be reorganized as a small business providing services to the firm. In this way, many parts of a large SOE could be separated off into small firms or microbusinesses, which would then be energized to grow and take on other business. At the enterprise level a special unit in the SOE could function as an "internal incubator" to spin off these small service businesses or parts suppliers.

---

8. Such micro spin-offs were part of the restructuring program at the Ispat-Karmet Steelworks in Kazakhstan that was supported by the European Bank for Reconstruction and Development (EBRD) and the International Finance Corporation (IFC).

Local governments can help reform the investment climate for SMEs by simplifying, making transparent, and expediting the process for new business start-ups and spin-offs. With a clear public mandate from above to improve the local business climate, associations of small businesses can be encouraged to bring pressure on local governments from below.

Another element of an enabling investment climate is empowerment through education and training. The managers and entrepreneurs of new start-ups or spin-offs will largely be people who have already been working but who have little experience with running a market-based enterprise. Hence I must emphasize the importance of retraining people for micro-, small-, and medium-size businesses. Public or private education organizations and extension services need to address this challenge. The new information technologies for distance learning could be helpful in this regard.

Exit: Creative destruction. In his grand vision of market-driven development, Joseph Schumpeter used the phrase "creative destruction" to emphasize that birth and death are equally part of economic life. At the level of society as a whole, there is a process of "creative destruction" that carries from one stage of reform to the next. The creative institutional solution at one stage may become an impediment that needs to be transformed to move on to the next stage.

Creative destruction is also needed at the micro level of the firm. When creating opportunities for jobs is such a primary imperative, it might seem contradictory to emphasize the need to develop workable bankruptcy procedures. But jobs maintained only through subsidies that postpone bankruptcy are sterile jobs: they lead to no new growth, and they cannot multiply. By streamlining the mechanisms for restructuring or recycling the old assets, and by retraining the workers, many more new jobs—real jobs—can be created.

Since I am sure you have heard enough general lectures from Western economists about strengthening bankruptcy, let me make two specific points. One of the social virtues of restructuring big companies into a number of medium-size companies (e.g., spin-offs) is that it facilitates enforcing the hard budget constraint by making the smaller companies "bankruptable," whereas the original large SOE could play the "too big to fail" game. Middle managers face a tradeoff: the spin-off allows them greater freedom and capacity to innovate, but the budget constraint is hard. The government needs to tilt the balance in favor of the new firms.

The second point is that when companies go into liquidation bank-ruptcy, the physical premises of an old factory can be turned into an "industrial park" for new small businesses started by entrepreneurial middle managers, engineers, and workers, using part of the old space and some of the old equipment and employing some of the old staff. That also preserves some of the viable bits of the old firm's organizational capital. In a transition economy bankruptcy and new start-ups should not be two separate processes but, whenever possible, two sides of the same coin. After a few success stories, this form of bankruptcy, together with start-ups, will begin to relieve the social pressures against bank-ruptcy and make it easier for the restructuring process to go forward.[9]

Enabling SME growth: Business services. Removing restrictions and red tape on small business start-ups is only part of the task of improving the investment climate. Large firms might try to internally supply many of their own needs, but small and medium-size businesses everywhere need certain complementary services that they cannot afford to staff inter-nally. These include accounting, auditing, valuation services, marketing, design, engineering, training, information processing, equipment repair, and, of course, financing.

In the past there was little role for services such as marketing and exter-nal auditing, and few of the services that were available were provided by independent small companies. Hence one should see the service sector as a source of growth in its own right, as well as a necessary part of growth in the SME manufacturing sectors. Some of this growth in the service sector can come from the entry and expansion of international service firms. But there is no reason why much of the service sector growth cannot come from spinning off service units and staff functions from large companies as they become less vertically integrated. The service units could become independent businesses, contractually pro-viding services to their original unit and also supplying a broader range of customers.

Enabling SME growth: The financial sector. I do not need to remind you about the unfinished agenda in the financial sector, with its nonperforming loans and the continuing need to restructure financial

---

9. Some economists might complain that this sort of liquidation emphasizing new jobs for the old staff is "inefficient" and that the assets should be auctioned off to the highest bidder. But that sort of narrow "textbook efficiency" may never get beyond the textbooks if social pressures block such liquidations.

institutions to operate in a market economy.[10] Instead, I would like to emphasize small business finance—both trade finance and longer-term finance—since small businesses will be an important driver of new growth and job creation. When small firms are spun off from SOEs and TVEs, the parent firm can usually provide some finance or can directly supply some of the assets on a lease basis and some of the inputs on a credit basis. But the accelerated development of banks to finance small and medium-size companies is necessary for broader growth.

Commercial lending on a sustainable basis is not a practice that can be installed quickly by following a checklist. Seasoned experience and mature judgment are key elements in the banking business, and those human skills take years to develop. It is important to maximize horizontal learning between the banks that successfully develop the SME banking business and the banks that are lagging behind.

Other Components of the Investment Climate

Let me now turn to the infrastructure that complements private sector growth, the regulatory mechanisms that provide the framework for growth, and some of the emerging corporate governance issues.

Infrastructure services. Large SOEs or TVEs are often highly integrated, economically and socially, with their own sources of power and their own facilities for housing, schools, health care, and recreation. The strategy I am suggesting—one of restructuring large firms, where appropriate, into a group of medium-size firms—requires that this infrastructure also be restructured so that the spun-off units will still have access to infrastructure services. In part this might mean privatization (as in the case of apartments) or transfer of the function to the appropriate level of government (in the case of health services or schools).

Small and medium-size businesses have to depend on these infrastructure services being supplied externally from the beginning. As China moves from the reforms in agriculture and the TVEs to the third phase of growth driven by the private sector, in which private SMEs will be the main sources of growth, the infrastructure of telecommunications, power, and water will need to keep pace with (or even lead) the new

---

10. See the World Bank's new Policy Research Report, *Finance for Growth: Policy Choices in a Volatile World* (World Bank 2001e).

growth. Pragmatism toward partnerships (both public-private and Chinese-foreign) and experimentation with different approaches will help achieve this end.

Regulatory policies. Full opening to private sector growth does not mean that the government must fade away. Instead, the government will need to change its function from that of owner and manager to that of regulator and referee. Industrial and developing countries display a rich variety of effective regulatory structures. Within this variety, however, we find common policies that should inform and guide regulatory experimentation and practice.

You know about the World Bank's role in financing infrastructure, but we also have a role in encouraging the creation of knowledge in that field. We are working to strengthen knowledge institutions in developing countries so that those institutions can learn more effectively from *any* source—from their own experience, from the practical experience of others, and, yes, from experts at the World Bank. The World Bank Institute has helped develop just this type of learning institution in China: the Research Center for Regulation and Competition (RCRC) of the Chinese Academy of Social Science. The RCRC gathers knowledge about infrastructure regulation and competition from practitioners and academics around the world (including from the World Bank) and then works with the government to apply this knowledge to Chinese circumstances. The RCRC is currently working with the government on telecommunications reform, railway reform, and the reform of administrative law. In the past two years it has published 6 books and over 20 articles in Chinese journals and has conducted training programs for academics and practitioners across the country.

Corporate governance issues in SOE reform. The reform and transformation of SOEs is one of the key unfinished challenges, and much depends on meeting it. But we must recognize that a simplistic plan for SOE reform based on floating shares on public stock markets is not going to drive deep, long-term restructuring, nor is it going to stop the practice of bailing out companies seen as "too big to fail." The diverse ownership arising from public flotation is unlikely to provide for strong decision-making, and the legacy of the "iron rice bowl" in China will add to the reluctance to see big firms fail which is powerful in most countries (as in the United Staes with Lockheed and Chrysler).

The focus of SOE reforms should lie elsewhere. The SOEs from the old nonmarket economy are often too big. Through spin-offs and break-ups, the average size of companies should be reduced (even if the new firms later recombine in new ways). One possibility is for the SOEs to be broken up into groups of contractually related medium-size enterprises. Vertical pyramid structures, with the parent companies having control of the child companies are less likely to be attractive, since the point is to decentralize control to foster innovation and new combinations.

How might this improve the management of companies? First, the smaller units would have real freedom to strike new contracts with other firms and in other markets. Second, real restructuring is much easier in smaller units than in large ones. Moreover, in smaller units it is easier to rebuild the workplace culture from that of a state enterprise to that of a market-oriented firm. Third, if a large SOE were broken up into medium-size parts, the chief executive officers of the new smaller enterprises would be, on average, middle-aged or younger entrepreneurial people rather than older people on the edge of retirement. This infusion of new blood into a leadership role would promote more restructuring. It would also bring a longer-term perspective, particularly when coupled with stable share ownership. The older top managers in the large SOE might have the "age 59 problem" resulting from their imminent retirement, while the younger CEOs, managers, and technical staff in the medium-size units would look forward to more years with the company before retirement.[11]

Social Protection and Pension Reform

The building of a deeper market economy will highlight the need for a different kind of social protection. The role of social protection in a market economy is sometimes misunderstood. First, the purpose is to protect people, not enterprises. Second, it is not a "welfare program" for those without any other means of support. At the end of the day, the best social protection for the great mass of society is a growing economy.

---

11. The "age 59 problem" was seen in the Russian reforms. "For instance, privatisation without restructuring left the enterprises in control of people in their 50s; the absence of well developed capital markets meant that they were unlikely to be able to reap the benefits of any improvement in enterprise performance upon retirement (by selling shares at increased prices). Even in the case of listed shares, the vagaries in share prices meant that extracting returns from higher share price as a result of improved corporate performance was a highly risky matter; there were far more certain returns from asset stripping. Breaking enterprises up would have put more of them under the control of younger managers, who would have had longer time horizons" (Hussain, Stern, and Stiglitz 2000: 249, fn. 15).

Thus, social protection should be seen as a way to facilitate change and learning—not as a way to cover the costs of failing to learn or change. Furthermore, social protection should go well beyond the passive role of a safety net to a more active role of retraining—to "bounce" people back into the productive economy so they are empowered to shape their own economic lives rather than grow dependent on a welfare system.

After their years of economic work end, the elderly must depend for income on family support informal systems or on more formal pension systems. China's pension system for state-sector employees, which has traditionally been financed and managed by enterprises, has become dysfunctional with the marked deterioration in the financial position of the state sector since the mid-1990s. The system imposes a heavy financial and administrative burden on enterprises and hinders their restructuring. Moreover, it is not able to pay pensions to retirees on time. China's leadership recognizes these problems. The management of the system is therefore being transferred from enterprises to city governments, while single-source financing by enterprises is being replaced by three-way financing by enterprises, employees, and the government.

The work on designing the new pension system is making substantial progress toward putting in place the main requisites of a good pension system. But the new system is rendered nonoperational by the massive overhang of unfunded liabilities from the old system. The result is an awkward hybrid of old and new. The partial funding of future pensions provided in the new system may not work in practice because all of the current contributions are used to pay current pensions. Moreover, most cities are too small to provide adequate risk-pooling under the city-based system, and the aim of building a province-level system remains to be implemented.

A successful transition from the old system to the new one will depend on formulating a concerted strategy to tackle the change, before the financial overhang of unfunded liabilities increases too dramatically. Possible sources of funding for pension liabilities include proceeds from the sale of state assets (including equity stakes in state enterprises), general tax revenue, and the issuance of bonds.

Increasing Internal Integration and Attacking Poverty

A second major item on China's growth agenda is to increase internal integration and attack poverty directly, to ensure that growth reaches the remaining poor people.

The Multiple Dimensions of Poverty

Before taking up the issue of how China can best attack the remaining concentrations of poverty, we must first form an understanding of what poverty is. Traditionally, economists and others have focused heavily on income poverty: those with household incomes below a certain cutoff level are regarded as poor. But income is just one dimension of poverty, albeit a very important one. Poverty is a multidimensional phenomenon encompassing various types of deprivation that constrain the lives of poor people.

At the World Bank, we often express this idea using the concepts set out in *World Development Report* (WDR) *2000/2001: Attacking Poverty.* That report drew heavily on developments in our empirical and theoretical understanding of poverty in the 10 years since our previous *World Development Report* on poverty, as well as on interviews with tens of thousands of poor people around the world on their understanding of the fundamental elements of poverty. The 2000/2001 *World Development Report* defined poverty as consisting, broadly speaking, of three key features of people's lives:

- *Lack of opportunity* to participate in and contribute to economic growth and development

- *Powerlessness* concerning key decisions that affect their lives

- *Vulnerability* to economic and other shocks, such as disease or injury, crop failures, and macroeconomic recessions.[12]

Other approaches have also emphasized the multidimensionality of poverty, while expressing it somewhat differently. An important example is the International Development Goals, to which most of the world's governments have subscribed through the United Nations and other forums. In setting goals, we also implicitly embody definitions of poverty. These international goals propose targets for poverty reduction—not just in terms of raising the incomes of poor people but also in terms of improvements in health and education. The international community recognizes that by reducing illiteracy and child mortality, we are striking blows against crippling dimensions of poverty, whether or not income poverty falls. Better health and education are thus ends in them-

---

12. To put it positively, the WDR strategy for attacking poverty focuses on ensuring that poor people have *opportunity, empowerment,* and *security.*

selves. They are, of course, also means to improve on other dimensions: reducing illiteracy has productivity payoffs and will, in fact, reduce income poverty and improve health.

Although we find our three-part WDR categorization very useful—and indeed, I will draw on it later in what I have to say—the most important point to establish at the outset is that focusing on income alone is not enough, either for an understanding of the meaning of poverty or for the construction of policies to fight it.

Improving Data on Poverty

Earlier, I outlined what we know about the poor in China. But there is also a good deal that we do not know, and one major step in attacking poverty will be to deepen and extend the base of poverty data available for informing policy. We have to know who and where the poor are. China has a well-established tradition of household survey data collection. Since the mid-1980s the National Bureau of Statistics (NBS) has fielded careful annual surveys in both urban and rural areas. In addition, roughly half of China's provinces augment this national-level effort with surveys at the province level, based on the same survey instruments as the national surveys. These data have fueled many insights used to guide policy for fighting poverty.

Yet, with improvements in collection and dissemination, data could achieve still more than they do now. Let us look first at data collection. The statistics cited in this speech mostly concern rural areas, in part because that is where the large majority of poor people are found but also because the monitoring and evaluation system for tracking rural poverty is better developed than that for urban areas. As the government has pointed out, China has a pressing need to develop poverty monitoring of comparable quality for urban areas. Of greatest concern, from a data standpoint, is the growth in the floating population of unregistered rural migrants now living in urban areas, who are completely missed by the current urban household survey. Given this trend, as well as the increased worker mobility that will come from further reform of state-owned enterprises, China will need to learn much more about the identity and characteristics of its urban poor. The urban poverty monitoring and evaluation system recently proposed by the NBS would go a long way toward filling this knowledge gap.

Second, let me say a word about data dissemination. In principle, the household data already collected can be used to track the evolution of poverty and inequality over time, as well as to compare levels in any particular year across provinces and sectors. To date, however, access to unit-record-level data from these surveys has been restricted, and results have generally been available only in the form of tabulations published by the NBS. In those cases when greater access has been granted, including to researchers at the World Bank, the outcome has been detailed analysis that helps policymakers design interventions to reduce poverty. Examples include many of the findings cited in this speech—for example, the success of poor-area development in reducing rural poverty (Jalan and Ravallion 1998a) and the characteristics and causes of chronic poverty and transient poverty in China (Jalan and Ravallion 1999). A review of the policy of restricting data access would therefore be highly desirable. Beyond improving analysis, open access would improve the data itself by increasing the transparency and scrutiny of data collection and dissemination and involving researchers in that process.[13]

Expanding Opportunities for Lagging Areas and Excluded Groups

Improving data, then, is one important component of the poverty reduction strategy. The other components can be organized around the WDR trilogy that I mentioned before: opportunity, empowerment, and security.[14] First, let us focus on opportunity. The opportunity pillar of poverty reduction is closely related to a focus on income growth, but it represents much more than that. It emphasizes the need to ensure that poor people have real possibilities to participate actively in development—or, to use Amartya Sen's language, that poor people are able to develop and use their capabilities. This focus is fundamentally different from one concerned only with outcomes, such as the level of income or even the education of an individual.

Income disparities and geographic poverty traps. The review of the evidence in the preceding section has made it clear that for all the progress China has made, absolute poverty remains a major challenge. Not only are there large disparities between rich and poor households and regions, but there also appears to be no tendency toward convergence of incomes. In fact, the data show the opposite: the incomes of poor people rose at barely *half* the overall growth rate in the 1990s. Specifically, while the overall growth rate in household income per capita was 7 percent, the mean growth rate for poor people has been a more modest

---

13. Indeed, this is what has happened in India in recent years. For more detail on data issues, see Stern (2001).

14. This section draws heavily on World Bank (2001a).

4 percent. For poor people in most countries in the world, of course, an average annual income growth of 4 percent annually would be a great improvement—yet in China that rate was just one-third of the 12 percent growth rate that the wealthiest group enjoyed. Nor are these segments of the population unique: as Figure 3 shows, growth rates rose steadily with income all along the income distribution. This trend was reversed only temporarily in 1993–96, when unsustainably high grain prices lifted the incomes of rural households.

Geographic differences explain much of this divergence between poor and rich: not only are rural areas poorer than provinces nearer the coast, but they grew more slowly overall in the 1990s. Careful analysis of the micro evidence strongly suggests that this divergence is explained in part by geographic poverty traps. That is, once we take into account individual and household characteristics, geographic characteristics can lead to a divergence in incomes. Take two otherwise identical households, one living in a poorly endowed area, the other in a richly endowed area. Over time, as World Bank research has shown, the latter will typically escape poverty much more quickly than the former. For example, research using panel data from four southern provinces estimated that living in a mountainous area rather than on the plains cost a household between 1 and 2 percentage points of consumption growth per year, even after taking many other household and geographic variables into account (Jalan and Ravallion 2000). The panel data for this test were collected in 1985–90, and as more data become available, further work will be necessary to update these results and ensure that they do not just reflect post-reform adjustment to a new equilibrium. Nevertheless, what evidence we have indicates strongly that the remaining poor provinces face significant barriers to their development.

Policy implications. The evidence on who the poor people are and where they are suggests that there are large potential gains to expanding further the opportunities available to China's remaining poor. In the overall rural strategy, this means fighting poverty by doing what is necessary to encourage both off-farm employment in rural areas and agricultural growth. Unlike countries such as India, China has managed to generate substantial off-farm employment opportunities without migration on the scale seen elsewhere. Migration is growing as an option for off-farm employment of rural labor: about 12 percent of rural workers are now employed outside their township of origin compared with perhaps 2 percent in 1989. Even a modest amount of out-migration can increase welfare in rural areas by taking pressure off the labor market, providing remittances to rural households, and improving commercial ties between poor areas and the rest of the country. But the scale of poverty and the pressures on towns, taken together, indicate that most of the poverty gains will have to come from providing expanded opportunities to the much larger number of farmers and laborers who remain in rural areas. There are several implications.

- *Improving rural infrastructure*, especially transport, is key for promoting both off-farm employment and agricultural growth. Evidence has shown that such actions as investment in rural roads may be essential to this process. For example, the study, cited above, of growth in four provinces showed that when other characteristics are held at their average value, counties with less than 6.5 kilometers of roads per 10,000 people enjoyed no consumption growth at all.[15]

- *Promoting development of off-farm SMEs* in poor counties is another avenue for accelerating income growth. Opportunities for improving the sector include reducing the barriers to entry for new enterprises, reforming the ownership and management of lagging TVEs (for example, by shifting them to the private sector where appropriate), allowing the weakest TVEs to go bankrupt, and encouraging others to form joint ventures with enterprises from more developed areas.[16] As I argued earlier, an important avenue for growth may be small businesses spun off by TVEs—transport businesses, for example, or vehicle repair shops. Such spin-offs can do much to encourage the dynamism of the off-farm sector.

- *Improving and expanding microcredit* would help farmers and micro-entrepreneurs overcome a major barrier to growth, although it should not be expected to reach the poorest groups directly. To expand access to microcredit, the government may need to improve financial management, supervision, monitoring, and internal auditing of

---

15. Jalan and Ravallion (2000) note that 6.5 kilometers of roads is within one standard deviation of the mean for all counties in the sample.

16. As a sector, the TVEs are not likely to be as viable as a source of employment growth in the lagging areas as they were in earlier growth provinces. In particular, manufacturing TVEs may be less of an option in sparsely populated areas that suffer from severe transport and communications problems than they were in the coastal provinces. Even in these less populated areas, however, there may be scope for SME growth in service industries. One might note, only a little facetiously, that fewer and fewer Chinese people have long hair than in the past and that more and more have cars—leading to increased demand for barber and auto repair shops. Policy needs to make room for the growth of providers in service sectors like these.

microcredit schemes while also experimenting with devolution of responsibility for implementation to grassroots organizations.

- *Expanding educational opportunity* is essential. It is not always feasible to set the same educational attainment goals nationwide, given the considerable constraints in the poorest areas, but education policy needs to be designed in such a way as not to exacerbate problems of social exclusion. The Ministry of Education's national implementation plans for achieving universal basic education raise some concerns on this score. Whereas it would require nine years of education for all students in most of the country, it sets the minimum at only three to four years of education in the poorest areas, creating what seems to be a very large discrepancy.

- *Raising agricultural productivity* in the poorest regions is another priority. Even though the growth of off-farm incomes is important, agriculture will continue to be the mainstay of the rural economy for some time to come. But mountain agriculture in the poorest regions suffers from low yields and poor market timing, making competition with higher-yield areas difficult. Better crop choice and improved technology could help greatly. These could be spurred by a government effort to increase funds and establish or expand programs for training, access to technical investment information and physical investment in land improvement such as terracing and agricultural research that specifically address the problems of mountain agriculture.

- *Development programs for poor areas* have been an important direct intervention for poverty reduction. World Bank research indicates that, where implemented, these programs have raised growth rates significantly in poor counties, by perhaps 1.0 to 1.5 percent, and that they earn quite reasonable rates of return of perhaps 12 percent (Jalan and Ravallion 1998a). Programs of this kind that both support agricultural development and invest in education, health, and migration assistance can have particularly high payoffs.

- *Providing assistance with out-migration* from rural areas is an important complement to, although not a substitute for, all these efforts to promote rural development. Migration will have to be of a scale and on a time frame consistent with the capacity of cities to absorb the migrants. But even within those constraints, it is an important equilibrating mechanism and a means of including rural areas in dynamic urban growth. Because migration is both costly and risky for poor people, the government may have a role to play in reducing those costs and risks where that is developmentally appropriate.

In addition, China confronts the issue of how to reach poor people who live outside officially designated poor counties. As noted earlier, such counties are now home to only about half of all poor, and within the poor counties the large majority of people—some 85 to 90 percent—are not poor. As a result, much of the funding for poverty reduction is being diluted and is not reaching poor people through the current county-based system. A possible means of addressing this problem—one that I understand the government is now considering—would be to channel poverty reduction funding directly to poor townships, both within and outside the nationally designated poor counties.

Empowering Poor People

The second major dimension of poverty reduction is *empowering* poor people. This idea may sound very abstract or even utopian, but what it expresses is a deeply practical notion: that development happens fastest when poor people are able to influence the decisions that most affect their lives.

Recent Chinese history includes at least two major examples, each of which has played a key role in driving China's astonishing economic success of the past two decades. Each reform led to great improvements in incentives and helped fuel China's off-farm employment growth without large-scale migration. The first of these reforms was the creation of the Household Responsibility System. This innovation gave vast numbers of rural poor people control over key decisions regarding the production of agricultural goods—control that they had lacked during the years of collectivized agriculture. The new policy marked a return to incentive-based mechanisms that were familiar from the past, carried out on land that had been family cultivated just two decades earlier. In this case, the reform was first experimented with at the local level and then deliberately introduced on a national scale. This change dramatically improved agricultural productivity; annual growth in grain yields nearly doubled, to an average 5.7 percent for the 1978–84 period. The result was the first great wave of reform-era poverty reduction, as well as the release of labor for off-farm production.

The second major example is the growth of the township and village enterprises (TVEs) in the 1980s. By giving the TVEs greater responsibility for production and marketing decisions, the government released a dynamic force for growth and development that drove China's second wave of growth in the reform period. This innovation was built in part on the foundation of the collaborative behavior of the communes. But it also drew on earlier experience—in this case, experience with operating some of the factories two decades earlier. It also arose more spontaneously than the reforms in the agricultural sector, illustrating that when poor people are given the tools and opportunity to construct their own solutions to development problems, they will do so, often in ways unanticipated by economic policymakers or planners. Recall the quotation that I cited earlier in which Deng Xiaoping expressed the leadership's surprise at the rapid growth of the TVE sector. That quotation makes it clear that empowering poor people has to do not only with equity but also with efficiency, productivity, and growth. Those who are intimately involved in an activity, whether agricultural or industrial, will often have the incentives and knowledge necessary to allow them to find and exploit opportunities for greater productivity.

Another lesson from these examples is that empowerment can be either individual or social. In the first example, empowerment came from devolving power to the individual household, improving the incentives it faced, and giving it a greater measure of control over its production. In the TVE example, by contrast, we see that collective action can also be empowering to poor people and that sometimes it is by working together that they can best reach their goals.

Community involvement in infrastructure, schools, and natural resource management. There are other important examples of collective empowerment that improves development effectiveness. One is water users' associations, which, under the right circumstances, can be more effective in ensuring and maintaining a supply of clean water for communities than can the government alone. Similar organizations can help in the running of irrigation systems. Another example in which social organization has empowered poor people is the successful experiments with increased local control of schools. Through programs such as EDUCO in El Salvador and the District Primary Education Programme in India, committees of local parents have been given greater power to participate in and monitor the way schools are run. Our research shows that such parental involvement can lead to changes in education delivery and to better incentives that improve attendance of both students and teachers, with strong results.

In China the concept of empowerment is highly relevant to efforts to reduce rural poverty in the areas most threatened by natural resources degradation, particularly in hilly and mountainous areas and in the grassland regions. The government is well aware of the need for sustainable natural resource management in such regions and has devoted substantial resources to the problem through land conservation works and reforestation. Despite some successes, these programs have not realized their full potential. This is in part because the focus of investments has been on treating symptoms rather than underlying causes but also because—and here is where empowerment comes in—the approach has been too top-down, with inadequate participation by the beneficiaries. The Chinese researchers who identified this problem argue that a better approach would start from a clearer understanding of what is constraining the development of rural communities and how those constraints affect the behavior of communities and individuals. Once equipped with greater input from the communities, the government would find it easier to develop investment programs (perhaps community-managed ones) that will reduce rural poverty without degrading the natural resources needed for long-term poverty reduction.

Increasing the Security of the Poor

The third challenge, corresponding to the third broad dimension of poverty, is to increase the security of poor people by reducing their vulnerability to shocks. Poverty is not just a matter of numbers of people currently living beneath the poverty line, even if that is a sensible starting point. Beyond the number of officially poor, or even the larger number of absolute poor living on less than $1 per day, there are many more people in China who live just above the poverty line. These people are highly vulnerable to shocks that can easily throw them back into poverty. Research shows that a large share of all poverty in China—one-third to one-half, using poverty gap measures—is transient poverty (Jalan and Ravallion 1998b), which affects households whose average consumption over a multiyear period is enough to keep them out of poverty but who are sent below the poverty line in a given year by some adverse shock. And, of course, shocks that hit those who are *already* poor can be catastrophic.

Uninsured risk. Uninsured risk is pervasive in rural China and is emerging as a factor in urban China as well, particularly because of the growth of the floating population. Our detailed knowledge of the urban case is limited by the lack of data on these populations, but in recent years we have learned a good deal about risk in rural China.

What we have learned is that the rural poor are less well insured against shocks than are the non-poor. Motivated in part by the theory of risk-sharing, World Bank researchers have used household panel data for rural areas of southern China to study the effects of income changes on consumption, after controlling for aggregate village-level shocks (Jalan and Ravallion 1999). The same research also tested how well households were insured against covariate risk at the village level.[17] The tests were done separately for different wealth groups, and for households in poor and nonpoor areas.

The research provided convincing evidence that households were not able to insure themselves fully against negative shocks through savings, mutual assistance, or other measures. There is pervasive uninsured risk, both idiosyncratic (that is, household-specific) and covariate at the village level. And the less a household's wealth, the less well insured the household turns out to be.

The same research also suggests that unless credit and insurance options for poor people can be improved, one should not be surprised to see persistent inequality, and an inequitable growth process, in rural areas of China. Research has also shown that poor people in rural areas take costly actions to address risk. For example, they keep a higher share of their assets in relatively liquid form so that they can quickly convert it into consumption if the household is hit by an unexpected event (Jalan and Ravallion forthcoming). This precaution will tend to lower the returns that poor people earn on their already meager assets. But other risk-coping mechanisms are probably even more important. One such mechanism is a decision to stay put rather than migrate in search of better earnings. Although risk considerations might be expected to increase migration because it could diversify the household's earnings sources, our research on China has found the opposite: households that are already subject to greater risk apparently respond by forgoing migration opportunities. Migration would subject the family to the additional, and unacceptable, risk of losing farming rights to their plot of land.

Policy implications. The vulnerability/security dimension is a relatively new lens for looking at poverty. In China policy has historically targeted chronic poverty in lagging poor areas. But the factors behind chronic poverty can be quite different from those causing transient poverty. Transient poverty and uninsured risk have received relatively little policy attention, except in cases of shocks that affect a large area—an entire province, say. The inability of poor people to insure

---

17. Here, this is risk of events that affect all households in the village.

against smaller-scale risk, and the lack of government policy response to that risk, threaten the sustainability of poverty reduction efforts. What initially seems to be transient poverty can quickly become chronic poverty if the shock is severe enough.

These research results suggest that while arrangements for consumption insurance in rural areas of China do exist, they work considerably less well for households that are asset-poor. This strengthens the case, on both equity and efficiency grounds, for public action to provide better insurance. The specific form that such action should take in given circumstances is still an open question. A number of countries have been successful in using well-designed workfare schemes to provide cost-effective insurance for poor people. The key in designing such schemes is to set the wage rate at a sensible level—one high enough to provide real assistance to families but low enough to discourage the nonpoor from participating and also to discourage poor people from becoming dependent on the program over the long term. When the wage rate is set at the right level, poor people will turn to the scheme only when it is really needed. In such cases workfare can be a valuable safety net.

Promoting External Integration: WTO Accession and Trade

There are challenges to be met—and opportunities to grasp—as China opens up to international competition with its entry into the WTO. In the earlier stages of reform, China gained by opening up trade between regions that were relatively self-sufficient, in contrast to Stalin's hopelessly rigid and overintegrated system of production. These "gains from internal trade" were an important part of the growth story. China benefited from increased external trade as well. Indeed, China has made extraordinary reforms in its trade policies: tariff rates are a third what they were a decade ago, and nontariff barriers are a sixth of what they were (Lardy 2001). The remaining steps in arriving at a WTO agreement are relatively small compared with what has already been achieved, but they should yield further benefits.

Greater exposure to global competition will bring adjustment within sectors: better firms will succeed and expand, and many of the weaker firms will fail. There will be more bankruptcies (exits) and new start-ups (entries), and much greater labor mobility. In the United States, over a five-year period, one in three manufacturing firms disappears and is replaced by a new entrant. In open developing countries, turnover rates among firms are even higher. Much of the benefit of globalization comes from this dynamism: lots of new firms starting up, some succeeding, but many failing. For China to fully benefit from globalization, it needs institutions that support these birth and death processes (or "churning") of firms and that provide protection for workers. This increases the importance of tackling the older agenda for reform, such as restructuring and transforming the large SOEs and increasing the flexibility of the markets for land, labor, capital, and services.

As I have already mentioned, WTO accession holds out both the new challenges of global competition and new opportunities for gains from external trade on global markets. In any government that undertakes many simultaneous reforms, there is always the danger that pressures to protect old interests will lead to paralysis and stagnation. But WTO accession by China, like accession to the European Union by Eastern Europe, can be a great wind that fills the sails of reform and keeps the ship moving in the right direction.

Conclusion: The Challenges Ahead

China has made remarkable progress against poverty in the 23 years since reform was launched. The country's extraordinary growth has been a powerful driver of poverty reduction. It is unlikely, however, that growth by itself will fully overcome the poverty that remains, and it is equally unlikely that past reforms will be sufficient to sustain the growth momentum. With its agricultural and rural industrial reforms behind it, China now moves into a third phase of reforms as it strives to build a globally integrated market economy. The earlier reforms built on past memories and worked more by removing constraints and releasing pent-up energies than by building new institutions. But now the past is no longer prologue, and so the challenges are greater.

I have grouped the challenges into three categories: deepening the private sector, increasing internal integration and reducing poverty, and promoting external integration. It is urgent to get on with these tasks if the next phase of reform is to be as successful in raising living standards as were earlier phases. Within each of these categories, there are many institutional forms, and China, as in the past, will choose its own way.

Under the category of deepening the private sector, the fundamental principle in the new phase of reform will be the shift from old to new roles—from the government that serves as "parent," protecting and improving the firms, to the government that provides an enabling framework so that competition, both domestic and external, can be the driver for improving firms. In this new role, the government will also need to protect and help people who need to readjust to the new environment.

I would like to close with a few more thoughts about reducing poverty. In this speech I have suggested an understanding of poverty that extends well beyond a narrow income-based definition—one that encompasses not only human development in such areas as education and health but also the richer spectrum of opportunity, empowerment, and security. All these are crucial to development and continued poverty reduction. To make further progress in these areas, we will need a good understanding of who the remaining poor people are, where they live, and what barriers to development loom largest in their lives. A key step in this under-standing is careful analysis of good household data, which is why I have discussed the gathering and dissemination of this information.

Even with the research and experience now available, we know a con-siderable amount about the poverty that remains. For example, we know that the deep poverty of mountainous and western regions reflects spe-cial development problems, and probably significant geographic poverty traps; that for many poor people, poverty is compounded by ethnic mi-nority status or disability; that nearly half of all poor people live outside officially designated poor counties, raising the issue of how best to reach them; that poorer households have poor insurance against shocks; that transient poverty makes up a large share of all poverty; and that al-though empowerment of poor people has helped combat poverty in the past, it is still not a prominent enough feature of development strategies. But we need to know much more. The design of well-targeted transfers and of programs to promote growth in particular areas will depend on knowing more about the characteristics of the poor—their education levels, family size, health status, and gender breakdown, among other things. This type of information is generally available in many other countries, and we have found that it is crucial for understanding the complex interactions that affect the welfare of poor households.

Insights from analysis of available data make it clear that both growth and government transfers will be essential to reducing and eventually eradicating severe poverty in China. This conclusion has implications beyond the scope of today's speech; for example, it means that increas-ing tax revenues over the medium term is essential if China is to fund the transfers necessary to cushion the severest poverty.

Today, I have suggested some specific policies that build on the knowledge we have accumulated: policies to widen opportunities for poor people by stimulating growth of rural incomes and promoting human development, including basic schooling for all children; to empower poor people by involving them in management of schools and natural resources; and to increase their security through such means as workfare programs that provide a safety net.

Even as it rises to current poverty challenges, China will face new ones in the years ahead. With greater labor mobility, poverty is likely to become an urban problem once again—indeed, this is doubtless happening already, as will become clear when the household surveys are extended to the floating population. Another issue is the aging face of poverty: the system of the iron rice bowl protected the elderly in the past, but the shift away from lifetime association with a single enterprise will, in the absence of a more formal system of support for the elderly, increase rates of poverty in that group. In addition, China's increasing integration with the world economy will have effects that are hard to predict with any certainty. Even though our research shows that integration raises growth rates without systematically increasing inequality, different countries experience different effects from globalization. Finally, China will need to turn its attention to other non-income dimensions of poverty reduction, such as ensuring that the security of poor people is not threatened by deterioration in the social order. My experience with China over the years makes me confident that although these poverty challenges are great, this is a country with the dynamism and social cohesion necessary to address them. We at the World Bank look forward to working with you on them in the years to come.

Figure 2. Poverty Incidence in Rural China, 1996
(percent below $1/day)

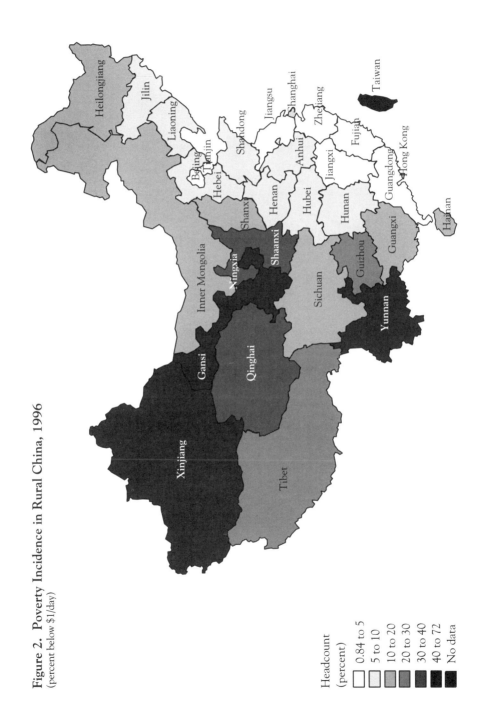

Headcount
(percent)

☐ 0.84 to 5
☐ 5 to 10
☐ 10 to 20
☐ 20 to 30
☐ 30 to 40
☐ 40 to 72
☐ No data

Figure 3. Growth Incidence Curve for China, 1990–99

Annual growth in income per person (percent)

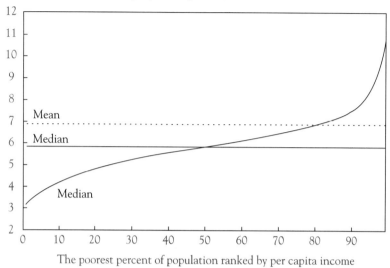

The poorest percent of population ranked by per capita income

Source: Ravallion and Chen (2001).

A Strategy for Development

Nicholas Stern

ABCDE Keynote Address, Washington D.C., May 2001

M y purpose today is to outline a strategy for development and to
draw some implications for the development research agenda. The
title I have chosen deliberately echoes Albert Hirschman's *The Strategy
of Economic Development* (1958) and his emphasis on processes rather
than prices and quantities. By leaving out "Economic" in the title, I do
not pretend to be broader or more catholic than Hirschman. But development research has unfolded in many directions since his pioneering
1958 book, and today the adjective "economic" might be given an interpretation too narrow for the strategy I will outline, one that draws
heavily on Schumpeter's majestic vision of the dynamics of a market
economy. I must mention, too, Amartya Sen, whose work has been
central to the broadening of perspective on the meaning of "development" and "poverty reduction." The title of his book *Development as
Freedom* (1999) embodies the key idea of development as the enhancement of individuals' abilities to shape their own lives. The direct and
indirect influences of Hirschman's, Schumpeter's, and Sen's understanding of the processes and objectives of development will be clear in the
strategy I will outline here.

Two pillars form the basis for this strategy of development: building an
investment climate that facilitates investment and growth, and empowering poor people to participate in that growth. The strategy is, in essence, a strategy for pro-poor growth. I will examine the key links
between investment climate and empowerment, as the strategic pillars,
and the goal of poverty-reducing development. The strategy for development will sound, I hope, very plausible, indeed almost obvious. But this
description is fairly new and is not universally accepted.

The word "investment" in the phrase "investment climate" will evoke
memories, for some, of the development philosophies of the 1950s and
1960s, when the emphasis was on growth through capital accumulation.
There was mistrust of the private sector and little mention of entrepreneurship or social inclusion. Development assistance was seen primarily

as the transfer of capital to the countries that had emerged from colonialism and aspired to join the ranks of industrial countries. Since those early days of development economics, we have, I hope, learned much.

My emphasis here will be very different from those earlier models and will be, first, on growth driven by the private sector and, second, on how to empower poor people so that they can participate strongly in the process of growth. Both elements are crucial for fighting poverty.

First, consider the role of the private sector. Not only is the private sector the main engine of aggregate growth, it is also the main provider of economic activity for poor people. Of the 1.2 billion people in the world who live on less than $1 a day, only a minute fraction work in the public sector. The growth of the private sector is therefore vital to the reduction of poverty. But that growth will not take place as a simple translation of investment into increased output. What the notion of "investment climate" captures instead is a Schumpeterian view of investment and growth—a view that what matters is not just how much investment takes place but what drives it, what are its effects—in particular, its dynamic effects on productivity and further opportunities—and what happens to the other factors of production and their productivity. In other words, it tries to capture the whole process of investment and growth, not just a simple snapshot at the point of investment.

Just as the concept of "investment climate" broadens our view of production processes in a useful way, so too have new insights expanded our understanding of poverty. We have moved to an ex ante rather than an ex post notion. Instead of simply asking whether a person's current income level classifies that person as poor, we ask whether, or to what extent, he or she has the capabilities and environment for action and success. Put another way, in the language of *World Development Report 2000/2001*, do people enjoy opportunity, empowerment, and security? This trilogy captures both the ex ante "freedom" notion of poverty and the idea that there are more dimensions of poverty than lack of income. To attack poverty involves, in large measure, empowering poor people to shape their own lives, through opportunities to obtain education and health care, through risk reduction and mitigation, and through participation in the key decisions that affect them and their families.

The Investment Climate

By "investment climate," I mean the policy, institutional, and behavioral environment, both present and expected, that influences the returns and risks associated with investment. The notion of investment climate focuses on questions of institutions, governance, policies, stability, and infrastructure that affect not just the level of capital investment but also the productivity of existing investments—indeed, of all factors of production—and the willingness to make productive investments for the longer term.

Seen in this broad way, the investment climate clearly depends on many different aspects of public and private action. It is useful to group these factors under three broad headings.

First are *macroeconomic stability and openness*. These embody the usual sound and sensible, if standard, economic prescriptions for macro and trade policy.

Second is a set of issues that can be grouped under *good governance and strong institutions*. These issues will be my main focus here. They include:

- Government institutions and behavior (including limitations on bureaucratic harassment, especially in the administration of regulations and taxes); the strength of financial institutions; the rule of law, including law enforcement; and the control of corruption and crime

- The effectiveness of the government in providing sound regulatory structures for the promotion of a competitive private sector

- The effective provision of public services or of the framework for such services, and the quality of the labor force.

Third is the *quality of infrastructure*, including power, water, transport, and telecommunications.

That is a long list, and it looks fairly comprehensive. Let us try to get more concrete by exploring what it means for economic activity at the micro level.

Why Is the Investment Climate So Important?

The key to improving the investment climate can be simply stated as improving the connection between sowing and reaping. This is not just a point about multinationals and foreign direct investors; it is, even more important, also a story of the local level, of the microentrepreneur, small business person, or farmer. Every day as they work, these people have to make decisions about the investment of their efforts and re-sources. A key to these investment decisions is the investors' sense of efficacy—their ability to get on with the job and see the rewards. Can investors carry out their efforts and reap the benefits, or will their investment be frustrated by uncertainty, instability, and predation? They will reasonably ask, "Why should I sow if I will not be able to reap a harvest?"

Government cannot guarantee the harvest against all the natural uncertainties of investment (although the social organization of insurance can mitigate the risks of natural adverse events). But it is a fundamental obligation of government to see that those who sow are not arbitrarily disrupted in their daily activities or robbed of their harvest by opportunistic human intervention. This is even more important than the protection of existing property because it is only by protecting the connection between investment and return that new property will be created.

Too often, we see societies that have stagnated at a low-level equilibrium because of a dearth of opportunities or incentives for investment. The government may protect the static accumulated wealth of the past (large landed property, for example), and in some countries it has acted as the "employer of last resort." But unless it takes steps to encourage entrepreneurial investment in the private sector, or at a minimum avoids stifling such investment, strong growth and poverty reduction are unlikely to ensue.

Consider the example of the Middle East and North Africa, a region that in the 1980s and 1990s suffered the paradox of high investment in human and physical capital juxtaposed with stagnation. Gross domestic product (GDP) per capita declined by 0.8 percent a year in the 1980s and increased only 1.1 percent a year in the 1990s. And yet rates of investment in both human and physical capital in the area have been impressively high. One of the primary reasons that such high rates of investment generated so little additional output is that the institutional structure of the labor market systematically misallocated labor. High government wages attracted the most qualified personnel to the public sector, and measures designed to protect existing employment made it difficult for entrepreneurs to start and sustain dynamic businesses.

In many countries of the world that have exhibited slow growth, those who might make entrepreneurial investments of energy and resources are left to be the prey of "bandits," both real and metaphorical. A never-ending stream of arbitrarily imposed rents, taxes, fees, and outright bribes and confiscations will drown even the most dedicated entrepreneurs, washing away all the energy and dynamism that power economic growth and lift people out of poverty. Creating a climate in which entrepreneurs and firms can do good business is crucial to encouraging the types of investment and economic activity that lead to long-term, sustainable economic growth.

This is especially true for small and medium-size enterprises (SMEs). Anyone who emphasizes the investment climate always risks being labeled a narrow-minded advocate for big business. But it is SMEs—and I include microenterprises under this rubric—that account for the majority of firms and a large share of employment in most developing countries, including (although to a lesser extent, on average) the transition economies. Furthermore, it is in SMEs, including farms, that most of the world's poor people are working. By enabling a dynamic SME sector in both rural and urban areas, governments can strengthen income-generating opportunities for poor people while reducing their vulnerability to economic risks.

There are several reasons for this emphasis on SMEs. First, in rural areas, off-farm SME employment can play a vital role in income growth and stability. In India, for example, our survey research shows that about a third of rural households' income comes from nonfarm sources, much of it from micro, small, or medium-size firms. The proportion of incomes is similar in the village of Palanpur, which my research collaborators and I have been following closely since 1974 and where our data go back to 1957. These incomes come from a variety of sectors, including commerce, manufacturing, and services, and they stem from regular and part-time wage employment, as well as self-employment. Village studies reveal that rural households value such nonfarm incomes highly, not only because they contribute significantly to overall income levels but also because they can reduce the exposure of households to potentially devastating income fluctuations associated with bad harvests. A strong investment climate, then, is central to the off-farm SME employment that can lead to higher incomes for the poor, as well as to diversification of economic risks.

Second, small-scale agricultural activities are themselves very vulnerable to an adverse investment climate. They can suffer as much as, or more than, other activities do from weak governance, malfunctioning infrastructure, and instability.

Third, we are likely to see an increase of some 2 billion in urban populations in developing countries over the next quarter-century. SMEs in urban areas will need to continue to provide employment opportunities for these rapidly growing urban communities.

Fourth, the experiences of the East Asian countries, notably Japan and China, and of the successful Polish and Hungarian transitions have shown us the great importance of urban and rural SMEs in overall economic development. In most development success stories, the growth of SMEs has been central, particularly in providing employment for poor people.

We must also recognize that the benefits of SME growth go beyond the provision of economic opportunity. Small firms give a breadth and depth to public voice. They have a stake in sound economic and political governance and thus can generate real forces for reform.

The Dynamics of Investment Climate

The new focus on investment climate differs in important respects from an emphasis on the ordinary notion of investment. In conventional theory, investment is expected to lead to diminishing returns. As more investments are made in one place, marginal returns decline, and new investment seeks other outlets. The concept of diminishing returns thus implies that "investment" is self-limiting in each use, as long as other key inputs, including technology, remain unchanged.

The investment climate, by contrast, can be positively or negatively self-reinforcing and thus can generate either prosperity or stagnation. Unlike the older stories of capital accumulation, the notion of investment climate tries to capture some of the external spillover effects, the complementarities, and the nonrivalrous public nature of improvements in governance and institutions. As the investment climate improves, the frontier of opportunity expands: existing investment becomes more productive, the rewards to productive behavior rise, the "animal spirits" (to use a term of which Keynes was fond) of entrepreneurs are encouraged, and the economy tends to attract more investment rather than less. These examples of the success of entrepreneurship and investment show other investors what is possible. But they also foster a greater understanding of and commitment to a sound investment climate, thus strengthening the political and economic forces that work in the direction of improving the investment climate. Because there will always be vested interests that benefit from the status quo, strengthening of the forces for change is a key part of the process.

A sound investment climate leads to the kind of sustained productivity improvements and vibrant entrepreneurship that induce a virtuous spiral of investment, growth, and poverty reduction. In contrast, where the climate for productive investment deteriorates, these processes work in reverse, and both replacement and new investments can suffer as a pernicious downward spiral sets in. The kinds of dynamic reinforcement or increasing returns I am describing may not apply as strongly in richer countries, where a greater part of the framework of a well-functioning market economy is in place, but they are unlikely to be entirely absent.

From this perspective, we may ask whether the reforms implemented by transition economies have increased or decreased people's sense of being able to determine their own lives. In too many cases, governments used the rhetoric of reform to justify all sorts of half-measures and misguided policies that only deepened people's cynical view that the more things change, the more they remain the same or deteriorate. The chipping away at public trust made later efforts to adopt real reforms—which rely so critically on credibility and consensus—that much more difficult. Much of the challenge for those whose job it is to promote development is to understand how to break free of a downward spiral.

Hirschman emphasized strongly the positive feedback dynamics of induced demand and learning in the investment process. For instance, he wrote that his "formulation of the development problem . . . calls particular attention to the fact that the use of different economic resources has very different repercussions or 'feedback' effects on the available stocks of these resources" (Hirschman 1958: 7). As he put it, investment in extraction of nonrenewable resources leads to the depletion rather than the augmentation of those resources and to little feedback elsewhere in the economy. By contrast, the investment of capital in a satisfactory investment climate can have significant positive feedback effects. Profits themselves generate the possibility of more investments; linkages to upstream or downstream industries will call forth complementary investments; and success will snowball by breeding confidence in investors and encouraging them to flock with other investors. Hirschman noted the crucial self-augmenting learning effects: "entrepreneurial and managerial ability . . . are resources that increase directly with and through use (much as the ability to play the piano or to speak a foreign language improves with exercise)." Finally he drew the implications for policy:

> The complementarity effect of investment is therefore the essential mechanism by which new energies are channeled toward the development process and through which the vicious circle that seems to confine it can be broken. To give maximum play to this effect must therefore be a primary objective of development policy. (Hirschman 1958: 43)

This effect has indeed played an important role in more recent models of growth with positive externalities from capital accumulation. It is part of the story of investment I am describing—but it is not the whole story. Also central to the process are the forces for change in building a stronger investment climate. We can see the investment climate as a further and crucial public good for all investors that is distinct from, although compatible with, the kind of investment externalities and complementarities emphasized by Hirschman and modern growth theory.

We can also see a clear difference between the earlier strategy of the international financial institutions (IFIs), which emphasized the transfer of capital to developing countries, and the strategy described here, which focuses on the investment climate. The volume of IFI investment will typically be a small part of total investment, and viewed in isolation from complementary external effects, it might exhibit diminishing returns. From the perspectives of dynamic learning and the investment climate, the purpose of IFI investment projects is not simply to transfer capital but also to create powerful demonstration effects (promoting "learning-by-watching" as well as "learning-by-doing") and to enhance the forces for changes in governance. These effects work on both productivity and the climate of expectations to help crowd in other investments. The emphasis on transition impact and demonstration effects has particularly characterized the approach of the European Bank for Reconstruction and Development (EBRD), where I was the chief economist for six years before coming to the World Bank. The EBRD has played a pioneering role both in the analysis of these ideas and in putting them into practice.

The other broad approach, which is particularly appropriate for the World Bank, is to focus on improving governance directly. Through its programs, the Bank works to promote the institutional adjustments, anticorruption measures, and policy changes that will change the rules and their enforcement, together with the way in which individuals and organizations behave and function, with the goal of directly improving the investment climate. As investors, whether domestic or foreign, come forward, they tend to demand more effective institutions, greater security, and constant improvements in the provision of public goods, which further enhances the quality of the investment climate. Without such changes in governance and institutions, economic decisions may continue to be dominated or blocked by those who are benefiting from (and who helped to create) the status quo.

Moving Forward

It is reported that Mark Twain said "Everyone talks about the weather but no one does anything about it." Today he might well ask, "Everyone is talking about the investment climate, but who is doing anything about it?"

The first step is to analyze the investment climate, notably through surveys. Strong analysis and identification of problems are not only a guide to reform but also a powerful spur to action. Striking figures can be cited to build public support for reform and help motivate a hesitant government. An example is the research carried out by the World Bank and the Confederation of Indian Industry (CII) that showed a large "tax burden" effect in the Indian states with a poor investment climate in comparison with the states with a good climate (CII and World Bank 2001). I will have more to say about this survey research when we turn to our research agenda. It is crucial to the ranking of key problems and to the identification of their nature, both of which will vary greatly from one location to another. Such information and ranking are crucial for setting priorities, as governments will not be able to tackle everything at once.

Good data and analysis, then, can help to pressure, motivate, and inform governments. The next question is, what exactly do we want governments to be motivated to do? We will not have simple answers to this question, as the response will vary dramatically by country. But one constant is that reforming the investment climate will require leadership and powerful advocacy, primarily from governments.

Leaders promoting reforms always face a fundamental problem, one that was given its classic expression by Machiavelli in *The Prince:*

> It must be considered that there is nothing more difficult to carry out, nor more doubtful of success, nor more dangerous to handle, than to initiate a new order of things. For the reformer has enemies in all those who profit by the old order, and only lukewarm defenders in all those who would profit by the new order . . . . Thus it arises that on every opportunity for attacking the reformer, his opponents do so with the zeal of partisans, the others only defend him half-heartedly, so that between them he runs great danger. (Machiavelli 1513, ch. 6)

The reformer's leadership lies in selecting and strengthening the best initiatives for reform (drawing on the type of analysis discussed above) and in taking positive action to weaken the obstacles erected by vested interests. It is interesting that Chandrababu Naidu, the chief minister of Andhra Pradesh, is fond of quoting this observation by Machiavelli. As a committed and successful reformer, he has a deep understanding of how tough reform can be.

But people who are not specially privileged may be also among those disrupted by the reallocations that are an integral part of reform. Social protection can play an important role here, but ultimately the best social protection for the great mass of society is a growing economy. Furthermore, changing the investment climate takes time; it is not a stroke-of-the-pen reform like eliminating a tax or fee. Thus, reformers not only have to argue their case strongly; they also have to prepare their constituents for the long haul.

The IFIs have a major role in supporting improvements in the investment climate. I will return to their important role as "agents of change" when I take up the topic of the research agenda in this area. At this point, let me note that the World Bank's focus on the structural agenda has increasingly led us to address the factors that together describe the investment climate, particularly as the Bank moves in the direction of long-term programmatic lending, as opposed to discrete projects or short-term adjustment loans. Programs addressing macro stability and openness are levers for changing the investment climate. Governance and institutional development programs are, or should be, in large measure concerned with the investment climate. They can influence how difficult or easy it is to register and start firms, to move goods in and out of the country through customs, and to pay taxes in a fair, predictable, and transparent way. The quality of different types of infrastructure—power, ports, telecommunications, roads, and rail, all of which call for far-sighted, market-oriented action—is another crucial part of the story. Programs to improve training and education systems enhance the quality of the labor force, in addition to being valuable in their own right. So, in short, I think there is a great deal that governments and IFIs, equipped with serious analysis of the issues in a particular country, can do about the investment climate.

Investment Climate → Growth → Poverty Reduction

I would now like to elaborate on the strong links leading from investment climate to growth and poverty reduction—not because the links are so surprising but because they are sometimes questioned and because the accumulated evidence is compelling.

It is widely agreed that the World Bank should help clients both with a "structural" agenda and with a "social" agenda. Some may be tempted to think of the structural agenda as for (hard-headed) growth and the social agenda as for (soft-hearted) poverty reduction, but this is the wrong way to view these issues. The social agenda of delivering public services, providing effective social protection, and empowering the poor to participate can contribute strongly to growth. And the structural agenda— although aimed directly at improving the investment climate—is vital for poverty reduction. We are not interested in investment or business development solely for its own sake. Rather, there is powerful evidence that the investment climate is a crucial ingredient for growth *and* for poverty reduction.

What is the evidence? First, consider the connection between the investment climate and growth. Developing countries that are improving their investment climates as part of globalization are clearly doing well. The top tier (about one-third, including China, India, and Mexico) of developing countries, as measured by moves towards liberalizing and expanding investment and foreign trade, did well in the 1990s, while the rest of the developing world as a whole did poorly. The expanded investment and trade stemmed partly from liberalization but also from infrastructure investment and streamlining of government regulations. The factors contributing to success varied among the countries in this group, and the style of reform was very country-specific, but all the countries showed real movement on some dimensions. By contrast, a number of studies have shown that Africa's low involvement in international trade has been influenced strongly by an unattractive investment climate— notably, by poor and deteriorating infrastructure and governance and by conflict. Among other large countries that have performed less well—including, for example, Russia and Pakistan— severe problems with property rights, the rule of law, and governance have been prominent.

The second link is that between growth and poverty reduction. On average, there is a close relationship between growth of per capita income and growth of incomes of the poor (although not all growth is equally "pro-poor," as we will see in the next section). Among low-income countries, Vietnam provides a clear example of this link. It made strong progress in its investment climate between 1992 and 1997, a period during which growth accelerated. Survey evidence shows that poverty dropped sharply: of the poorest 5 percent of households in 1992, 98 percent were better off five years later.

In some cases, members of poor households obtain employment in the formal sector firms that expand in a good investment environment. But benefits for the poor go well beyond this. A good investment climate is also beneficial for the informal sector, which usually employs far more people. Furthermore, formal sector investment and employment generation create new demand for informal sector expansion and for more farm output at better prices. In the successful reformers, increases in agricultural productivity and farm income have gone hand in hand with the generation of off-farm employment opportunities. China provides a striking example: the movement from communes to household operations led to dramatic increases in agricultural productivity in the early 1980s, with immediate consequences for poverty reduction. Very soon afterward, driven by the township and village enterprises, off-farm employment began to grow rapidly. Its growth has averaged more than 12 percent annually over the past 15 years.

I have given prominence in my arguments here to SMEs, but it is important to emphasize that in fast-growing economies large and small firms tend to prosper and cluster together. The task is to create a good investment climate for both categories of firm.

We are steadily learning more about all these links, not only by making comparisons across countries and time periods but also by comparing regions within countries. Much of what goes into the investment climate has to do with local institutions and policies, and in large countries these can vary substantially across regions. I briefly mentioned the CII– World Bank research in India. Because the investment climate varies greatly across states, the impact of macro reform on poverty also varies. Our recent survey of manufacturing firms that ranked 10 states according to their overall investment climate also found a similar ranking for poverty reduction by state (CII and World Bank 2001).

Empowerment ➜ Poverty Reduction

At the outset, I outlined a strategy for development and poverty reduction that is based on two pillars: investment climate and empowerment. A favorable investment climate can generate strong growth, and where there is growth, poverty reduction is likely. But it should not be taken for granted, because not all growth is equally pro-poor. The second pillar of empowerment and investment in people focuses on such questions as how educational and health services and social inclusion can enable poor people to take part in the process of growth and development.

At this point I should emphasize that poverty reduction is more than increasing income. Empowerment is both an inherent part of and a means for poverty reduction. Empowerment can indeed be an instrument for increasing income and for enhancing the assets, human and physical, of poor people. But it is in fact a broader notion, one that refers to the ability of people to shape their own lives. As such, it is an integral component of the standard of living—a message that we heard very clearly through the World Bank study *Voices of the Poor* (Narayan and others 2000), which drew on surveys of more than 60,000 poor people in over 60 countries. This perspective has also moved to center stage in the literature on the meaning of development, notably in the work of Amartya Sen. These broader notions of development and the role of empowerment were taken up in *World Development Report 2000/ 2001: Attacking Poverty* (World Bank 2000e).

Let me focus on three types of investments that are of particular importance in empowering poor people: investments in education, in social protection, and in participatory processes and social and economic inclusion.

Education. Basic education is critical to participation and productivity in economic life. A healthy, literate labor force will both increase the amount of growth realized from establishing a sound investment climate and strongly reinforce the poverty reduction benefit from that growth. The example of education clearly shows that the two pillars of investment climate and empowerment are closely connected and support one another.

We know, of course, that the promotion of education usually goes far beyond supplying resources. Just as important is the organization of the delivery of education and other public services. This is an area in which communities around the world are innovating, and there are many examples of exciting new initiatives. Often, these are more decentralized than past approaches, and local control and parental involvement are emerging as prominent themes. In these cases, the means of supplying education itself demonstrates the role of empowerment.

To take just one example, El Salvador's Community-Managed Schools Program has been expanding education in rural areas by enlisting and financing community management teams to operate schools. These teams, which are made up of parents and are elected by the community, have the responsibility, and the necessary power, for hiring and firing teachers and for equipping and maintaining schools. Their experience demonstrates that community-based incentives can encourage teachers to perform better. In particular, these program schools have lower teacher and student absenteeism than do traditional schools. Similar effects have been observed in India's District Primary Education Programme (also supported by the World Bank, but conceived within India), which features very strong community involvement and incentives for girls' enrollment.

The role of education in increasing both empowerment and economic growth is most striking when we look at the evidence on the education of women and girls. Raising women's schooling levels allows them to participate more broadly and more effectively both in the economy and in policymaking, administration, and government. The effects are deep and wide-ranging. First and foremost are the direct implications for the standard of living of women themselves. But the broader effects are also profound, and they influence the functioning of the whole economy and society.

The evidence on these effects is extensive and powerful, as is illustrated by the examples and literature cited in the recent World Bank publication *Engendering Development* (World Bank 2001a). Recent research reveals that countries with more women in parliament typically have significantly lower levels of corruption, even after controlling for national income and other relevant factors such as the extent of civil liberties and the degree of trade openness. These findings suggest that women are an effective force both for good government and for business trust. But if women's participation in political decisionmaking is to increase, their educational and literacy levels must be raised. In brief, more girls need to go to school and to stay in school longer.

Greater women's empowerment and education yield significant benefits virtually everywhere. There is a powerful relationship between female education and overall health—for example, mothers' education increases children's nutritional status, life expectancy, and general welfare. Increasingly, as data from longitudinal studies accumulates, we see that many of these effects last into later life; the mother's education is an important factor in the age-specific mortality rates of her children well into their adulthood.

Increased investments in women's education, then, yield a healthier, more literate, more productive, and better-governed society in the long run. However one looks at the issue of development and poverty reduction, and certainly from the perspective of the investment climate and empowerment, the education of women and girls is an investment with outstanding returns.

Social protection. Social protection can be seen as a dimension of empowerment—of enabling people to make adjustments and bounce back from economic shocks. During the adjustment after an opening to foreign trade, some formerly protected activities will cease to be viable, and some workers and firm owners will lose their employment and their incomes, even as new productive activities open up. Social protection measures can smooth this adjustment. Such measures have to be tailored to country circumstances. While unemployment insurance can be important for formal sector workers, other approaches, such as public work schemes of the cash-for-work or food-for-work varieties, are much more likely to reach the very poor.

But we should see social protection as much more than a short-run palliative. It is an essential underpinning of a market economy, one that helps it to function well and to involve poor people in the opportunities it creates. Without good social protection, poor people may be unable to take some of the risks that are part of participation in a market economy—even when they stand to gain strongly and to build their assets in the medium term. From this perspective, social protection is indeed a crucial element of empowerment.

Participation and inclusion. The third dimension of empowerment I want to discuss here is participation and inclusion in social organizations— from self-help credit groups, to water-user associations, to health services and the governance of schools. Examples of the benefits of participation stretch across sectors and countries, and the powerful effects of community participation on public service delivery are increasingly recognized. I have already given examples from education, but the effects are seen everywhere. For example, in some countries where enforcement of environmental pollution regulation is weak, governments have provided local communities with reliable pollution data (see *Greening Industry*, World Bank 2000b). Poor people living in the vicinity of industrial polluters have then been able to negotiate better arrangements for compensation and cleanup.

It is these dimensions of empowerment—equipping, protecting, and including people—that strengthen the connection between growth and poverty reduction and turn growth into pro-poor growth.

We can now see the deeper connection between the two pillars of investment climate and empowerment. To use yet other metaphors, investment climate as a lens brings into focus those reforms that increase people's sense of opportunity; if they sow, they will then be able to cultivate and reap. But, in a basic sense, these reforms also empower farmers, workers, and local entrepreneurs and managers to be able to build assets and to take control of their own lives.

Empowerment should be a self-reinforcing process, like changes in the investment climate. But I think we now recognize that in some countries, many actions seen as reforms have had an adverse effect. In a number of cases they took away the old way of doing things without providing any replacement, leaving people disempowered and demoralized. Instead of the people participating in reforms, the reform process was captured by elites, and most people were left to glean what they could from the leftovers. In those countries the investment climate has tended to spiral downward.

A Research Program in Support of the Strategy

The pillars of investment climate and empowerment together provide the basis of a strategy for pro-poor growth. I hope that as such they are very plausible—indeed, convincing. But they are not yet standard, and they constitute a fairly new way of looking at the challenge of development. This means that they also provide a research program of work that has to be done if we are to better understand each of the elements and how they combine. I would like to turn now to what might go into this research agenda.

Analyzing and Measuring the Investment Climate

The hard-headed economists among you will be saying, "All these notions of investment climate and empowerment are splendid, but where are the analytics and data?"

Can we be analytical in assessing or measuring the investment climate? We can, and researchers have already gone a long way toward doing so. We are helping our clients develop the skills to evaluate the quality of the investment climate in their own countries through systematic surveys of private firms, with a particular focus on small and medium-size enterprises. This research has already demonstrated dramatically that a hostile investment climate hits SMEs the hardest. A central output of such research is the identification of the key problems in the investment climate.

An important example of this work is the joint EBRD–World Bank Business Environment and Enterprise Performance Survey, which polled nearly 4,000 firms in 22 transition countries (World Bank 2000f). The survey broke new ground in quantifying the negative impact of different forms of corruption on the performance of firms. It also demonstrated in a systematic way, beyond the flashy media headlines, the pernicious influence of powerful vested interests, including the so-called oligarchs, in distorting the investment climate in transition economies and undermining growth. Such surveys are a valuable tool, not for lecturing other countries about the virtues of our own systems (which have their own problems) but for giving domestic firms a way of letting their governments know about the day-to-day obstacles they face in running a business.

Let me also share with you the results of the survey of 1,000 manufacturing and software firms in India that I mentioned above. Through our FACS (Firm Analysis and Competitiveness Surveys) program, we worked with an Indian partner to investigate differences in the investment climate in 10 Indian states. We found that the costs to businesses of a poor investment climate—for example, an unreliable power supply, onerous regulations, and intrusive and disruptive visits from government officials—are high. For firms in poor-climate states such as Uttar Pradesh (which has a population of 166 million, larger than that of Russia, Pakistan, Bangladesh, or Nigeria), those costs are analogous to an additional tax burden of up to 30 percent, conservatively estimated, compared with costs in Maharashtra State.

On examination, it is not difficult to see how one could arrive at such a large cost estimate. A functioning power grid is a key requirement for a vibrant SME sector. India is fairly remarkable in that because of the poor quality of grid-based electricity, most SMEs that we surveyed have their own power generators. In Uttar Pradesh 98 percent of firms surveyed had their own generators (they had little alternative), whereas in

Maharashtra the figure was considerably better, 44 percent. It is striking to the economic theorist that firms surveyed in Uttar Pradesh, one of the poorest states in India, with very low wage rates, showed higher capital-output ratios on average than those in some of the richest states. The intrusiveness of government regulation also varied sharply across states; for example, firms in the states with poor investment climates were visited twice as often by government officials as were firms in states with good climates. Thus the variation in investment climate from states like Maharashtra and Karnataka, at the high end, to Uttar Pradesh and West Bengal, at the low end, is real and measurable. Not surprisingly, the states with weak investment climates enjoy less growth and have seen less poverty reduction than the good-climate group. Variations in the investment climate are a key reason why some states remain poor and struggling while others are beginning to win the fight against poverty.

This type of firm survey has a number of advantages: it is systematic; it covers a broad section of the economy; it is amenable to fairly structured analysis; and it can yield reasonably robust general conclusions. Another source of information is the direct experience of IFIs as participant–investors in the private sector. The International Finance Corporation (IFC) and the EBRD are examples of public institutions that work as private-oriented investment banks. One of the great benefits of their activities, in my view, is that people who are actually involved in financing and making investments are also thinking about how to improve the environment in which the institution is functioning—and their hands-on analysis is from the perspective of public policy, not the narrow self-interest of business. This action basis for economic policy is invaluable.

A major item on the research agenda, then, must be to expand the effort to understand and, to the extent possible, quantify the different elements of the investment climate. Surveys of firms should stand next to household surveys as a centerpiece of microeconomic research and statistics in developing countries.

Other Areas of Research on the Investment Climate

In addition to firm surveys, the investment climate lens brings into focus other areas where research is needed, on both the theoretical and empirical fronts. In a standard neoclassical growth framework, investment in physical capital is subject to diminishing returns. Yet the examples of successful reformers, from China to Chile, suggest that the returns to reforms in the investment climate can help power robust growth for years and even decades. Understanding what is going on in such cases is a challenge for research on the investment climate.

One strong possibility is that when countries launch credible investment climate reforms, they in effect propel themselves into a virtuous circle characterized by increasing returns. A better investment climate increases the number of profitable investments. These success stories can serve as evidence of the government's reform-mindedness, and they motivate other entrepreneurs to take a chance and commit themselves to investing. That activity in turn builds constituencies for change and deepens the society's commitment to reform, and the society accordingly adopts additional reforms that further improve the investment climate.

A second, and more direct, effect is that reforms in the investment climate induce an increase in the (quality-adjusted) supply of other inputs into production, such as skilled and unskilled labor, entrepreneurship, and technology.

A third effect is the learning/externality story of productivity enhancement that has become familiar from modern theories of growth. (Of course, the theories of learning-by-doing and learning-by-watching have been with us for a long time and are central to Hirschman's argument.)

Combining these effects, we see that the observed productivity of capital will not necessarily fall over time as its supply increases, and the country will thus seem to have overcome the problem of diminishing returns. Each effect would be welcome in a country that has stagnated in the past, and each probably plays its part in most actual cases. It would be useful to disentangle the stories theoretically and conceptually and explore their implications for policy and measurement.

On the empirical side, an initial part of the agenda for research on the investment climate is to understand better the effects of reforms in this area. In doing so, it is useful to consider more broadly what metrics we will use in assessing the success of reforms. Time-series of firm survey data will tell us whether investors are becoming less hassled and more optimistic over time as policies change and will even allow us to quantify how reforms are affecting obstacles and production. They will not, however, allow us to gauge the full effects of improvements in the investment climate on the larger economy. For example, a regulatory framework that prevented new firms from entering an industry might increase the satisfaction of the owners and managers of existing firms—

even as it reduced the dynamism of the economy as a whole. But there is, of course, a broader constituency of potential investors and of consumers, now and in the future. We need other metrics to measure the effects of investment climate on this broader group and on the economy as a whole.

An obvious measure is the overall medium-term growth of the economy and the increase in productivity of all the factors. I used this GDP metric earlier when I mentioned our research showing that the top tier of developing country reformers had grown much faster than other developing countries in the 1990s and faster even than the industrial countries. Growth in total factor productivity (TFP), though hard to calculate with precision (and a notion that has its conceptual problems), can also give us some insight into how the investment climate is changing over longer periods, or at least point to its effects. Indeed, it serves to differentiate the notion of the investment *climate* from the measurement of quantities of investment only. TFP growth will not capture the induced increases in capital and labor supply, but it will provide an indication of the extent to which the investment climate supports or hinders the process of combining factors into final products.

A second measure, albeit a crude one, is the incremental capital-output ratio (ICOR), which focuses more directly on the effects of investment itself. An earlier generation of development economists tended to view the ICOR as a well-specified function; although it increased with capital accumulation, it was assumed to remain constant for any given level of the capital-output ratio (at least with Harrod-neutral technical progress). But we know that in fact there are wide variations in the ICOR, depending on the degree to which the investment climate is conducive to productivity and growth. For example, in recent years Poland, with a relatively modest investment ratio, has grown fairly rapidly, whereas Russia has grown much more slowly despite higher investment ratios. (Recall that the growth rate of output is the investment ratio divided by the ICOR.) Put simply, the climate in Russia was not conducive to productivity either of capital or of other factors.

So these measures, when combined with the results of firm surveys, can suggest whether the investment climate is making a difference. Note that while we should recognize that this analysis is one of those that "labels the residual" from growth analysis, it does at the same time try to link it to the direct measurement of underlying phenomena that we have good reason to think are genuine drivers of growth.

Let us now turn to research on each of the broad components of the investment climate that I mentioned earlier: macroeconomic stability and openness, good governance and strong institutions, and quality of infrastructure. In each case, a great deal of "drilling down" into these concepts and ideas is required.

Macroeconomic policy and openness. We can feel reasonably confident that improved macro stability and greater openness will generate more growth. But in view of the crisis in East Asia in 1997–98 and its reverberations in Russia and Latin America, not to mention more recent trouble spots, we have much to learn from further research about the best policy mixes and time paths of domestic macro policies, exchange-rate systems, and capital account management. Furthermore, different successful countries have found their own way, with their own time paths, in generating growth from more open trade and more stable macroeconomic policies. The adjustment process is not always easy, and it has to be adapted to local conditions and be constructed and led by the country itself.

All this relates to the larger issue of making globalization more pro-poor. Many fear that globalization will sweep through countries carrying new riches to the already well off while leaving poor people in stagnant backwaters. Our job is to find and foster pro-poor growth policies that empower poor people to lift their own sails and catch this new wind. The World Bank's Development Economics group (DEC) is now preparing a policy research report on the topic of globalization and how it can be harnessed to propel people out of poverty.

Governance and institutions. The second research topic in this group, the role and building of good governance and strong institutions, is one of the newest and most active areas of research. In recent years the Bank has moved from barely being able to mention corruption to undertaking a major effort in research and in programmatic lending on this issue. Surely, little or no research is required to learn that corruption is a major impediment to both domestic and foreign investment. In many countries the age-old problem is the herculean task of cleaning out the public stables. In this, surely research can help. Tolstoy tells us that every unhappy family is unhappy in its own way. Each country with a corruption problem, too, seems to have its own story to tell. Research is needed to understand how corruption works, who benefits the most, and who suffers the most. This knowledge will allow governments to devise more effective anticorruption policies.

Closely related to the problems of corruption and governance is the issue of institutional development. Recent experience in the transition economies has taught us hard lessons about the importance of institutions. Fair, competitive, and stable markets will not arise spontaneously out of the confusion of the transition; they require supporting institutions to administer and enforce property rights, legal codes, economic regulations, and taxation of individuals and companies. Those who are benefiting from, or who have benefited from, the "real existing post-socialist system" will not necessarily push to complete the transition to a full market economy. Laws can be changed overnight, but the bigger challenge is to establish reasonable and responsible conduct and behavior that is consistent with a well-functioning market economy. Changing those behavioral habits takes understanding, positive examples, leadership, and time.

Where the organic processes of building institutions have been torn apart by civil conflict, the ground is poisoned for future investment. The Bank is undertaking a new research program, led by Paul Collier, on the economic roots of civil conflict (including lootable natural resources and land pressures), in accordance with the old wisdom that "an ounce of prevention is worth a pound of cure."

No research in Washington or elsewhere can substitute for public resolve to fight corruption or can invent a way to "install" new institutions. Yet we think much can be learned from the experience of the industrial countries, and perhaps even more from successful reforms in developing countries. The Bank's early experience was summarized in Arturo Israel's 1987 book *Institutional Development*. In recent years, *World Development Report 1997*, on the role of the state (World Bank 1997b), set forth the initial results of research on corruption and on matching the complexity of proposed institutional reforms to the implementation capacity of the state. Several research studies published before the Annual Meetings in Prague in 2000—for example, *Anticorruption in Transition* (World Bank 2000a), *Helping Countries Combat Corruption* (World Bank 2000c), and *Reforming Public Institutions and Strengthening Governance* (World Bank 2000d)—summarized the Bank's progress in anticorruption and public governance programs since the 1997 *World Development Report*, focusing on the particularly vexing problems of corruption in the transition economies.

During the whole post–World War II period, the World Bank and the IFIs have been accumulating experience, from their successes and failures, on building institutions. Gathering, analyzing, and distilling policy recommendations from this experience is now an important research topic in the Bank. Indeed, *World Development Report 2001/2002* focuses on the institutional foundations of a market economy.

Infrastructure. The third research area relating to investment climate is the quality of infrastructure. Investors, both foreign and domestic, look to the quality of the power, transport, communications, and even financial infrastructure as an important complement to investment. Regulatory economics is now enjoying something of a renaissance as an outgrowth of the new information economics of moral hazard and adverse selection (pioneered by, among others, my predecessor as chief economist, Joseph Stiglitz) and also because of the new focus on increasing-returns phenomena such as network externalities. As Joe always explained, the correct perspective is not necessarily deregulation but sound regulation. In spite of this new birth of theory, political-economy problems still have to be solved in practice, as we were rudely reminded by the recent blackouts in California. Thus, our regulatory research program has had to walk on two legs. Bank researchers have mined the new regulatory economics for relevant theoretical insights, but they have also helped set up think tanks on practical regulatory issues in Latin America, Africa, South Asia, and China. Perhaps these new think tanks can be persuaded to give a seminar in California.

Research on Empowerment

The concept of empowerment also carries with it a rich research agenda. We have seen an extraordinary amount of experimentation with programs to empower poor people in different countries and at different levels. Think of the overwhelming variety of approaches to the organization and practice of educating children and adults, to reducing and mitigating risk, and to building social cohesion and inclusion. Our goal as researchers should be to understand how people have succeeded in empowering themselves—it is not for us to instruct people on their own empowerment. Rigorous evaluation has a large role to play here because it can help us cut through the thicket of promising approaches and disparate examples to discover which work best and under what circumstances. In an important sense, this research parallels the work on investment climate. In both cases our goal is to understand how governments can help the individual—or family, or firm—acquire the tools needed for success and how they can reduce the impediments to the fulfillment of the individual's (or family's, or firm's) potential.

More specifically, the research agenda for this second pillar can be derived from three important factors that affect empowerment and that I examined earlier: education and the delivery of other public services, social protection, and social inclusion and participation.

It should come as no surprise that *education* has been a strong area of research in DEC, the Human Development Network, the World Bank Institute, and other parts of the Bank. For example, we have taken the lead in evaluating the effects of some recent innovations in education, including the programs I mentioned earlier that have increased community involvement in school management in Central America and elsewhere. But a great deal remains to be done toward understanding the effectiveness of different approaches to schooling, not to mention adult education beyond formal schooling. And the problem is not limited to the education sector; many of the difficulties with education in developing countries are similar to those that impede the delivery of other public services such as health care. Indeed, the provision of basic services has such an important impact on poor people that it is likely to be the topic of a future *World Development Report* that will try to structure, summarize, and disseminate the research findings. Where we find successful practices, we will analyze and publicize them so that developing countries can learn from each others' experiences.

A crucial and central topic in current education research is girls' and women's education. As I noted above, education of girls and women has effects far beyond the expected gains in labor force productivity; for example, it improves the health outcomes of families, and it attacks directly the illiteracy and ignorance that constitute a key dimension of poverty. Some of the evidence has been brought together in *Engendering Development* (World Bank 2001a), which demonstrates the crucial role of women's and girls' education right across the economy. But much of the evidence, although wide ranging, is patchy, new, and tentative. *Engendering Development* is as much a research agenda as a research report.

Social protection is sometimes seen, mistakenly, as a charity program to alleviate the symptoms of poverty. We need a more active perspective on social protection as a springboard to help poor people bounce back from economic shocks. The dynamism of a market economy is based on risk-taking. Social protection is not only a safety net for those who drop out of the market; it should function as a part of a broader market economy that allows market participants who are less well off to take more entrepreneurial risks and to make the adjustments necessary for advancement. This perspective on social protection is a topic of active research in the Bank. But societies develop their own approaches to social protection, and here, as in any question of institutional change, we should be careful not to urge people to abandon the old ways when the path to the new ways is closed or obscured.

Finally, *participation and social inclusion* constitute a third dimension of empowerment. The principles of the Comprehensive Development Framework (CDF) have guided the Bank in a major reappraisal and recasting of its relationship with client countries. The basic CDF theme of "the country in the driver's seat" entails participation not simply by the government but also by the social organizations that reach down to the roots of society. Without that participation and inclusion, the new policies that might emerge from the CDF and the Poverty Reduction Strategy Papers would lack the broader ownership necessary for implementation. At the same time, country ownership does not imply automatic support for whatever is proposed. If we are serious about poverty reduction, we must concentrate our investments on the countries and programs that are generating the changes that can overcome poverty.

The IFIs as Agents of Change

This leads us directly to the next key area of research: how can the IFIs work as agents or catalysts of change to help countries implement the two-pillar strategy we have described? Our answer to this question is different from the one that would have been given 50, or perhaps even 10, years ago. Much has changed since the Bretton Woods Conference of 1944. The world economy has moved decisively toward greater integration, and the IFIs' understanding of development has broadened and deepened. We not only look beyond aggregate income to its distribution but also recognize that standards of living and thus development have key dimensions beyond income. With these broader goals, the IFIs have developed an appreciation of the crucial role of reforming policies and institutions.

Those of us who work in the IFIs are keenly aware of the changes and pressures that the acceleration of globalization brings for their role. How does the strategy of development outlined here give us a new purchase on this question?

I will argue that the IFIs do continue to have a role, but that it is a changed one which accepts the place of the private sector as the driver of development. The IFIs, as agents of change, should work to *create new opportunities*—that is, to help developing countries extend the frontier of what is possible. This should be the constant test that they apply to their activities, and it has at least three implications. First, it means that development assistance should have the effect of crowding in private investment—for example, through building a sound regulatory environment or upgrading the skills of the labor force—rather than substituting for such investment. Second, development assistance must be designed in such a way as to help build and raise the productivity of public resources rather than merely replace such resources. Third, IFIs should support projects that have powerful demonstration effects. These can be private sector projects (funded, for example, by the IFC or the EBRD) that are at the cutting edge of what the private sector can do or is willing to do and that thus demonstrate new opportunities. Or they can be public sector projects that can be replicated by other institutions and by other provinces or countries. The World Bank does indeed work both to find such projects and to encourage the learning process. There is a fundamental principle that should run through everything we do: *the IFIs should help finance the costs of change—and should not cover the costs of not changing.*

The IFIs should orient their work toward helping countries improve their investment climate while at the same time supporting country ownership of and commitment to reform initiatives. How do we do it? Serious research on this topic begins by recognizing that there *is* a conundrum in the whole idea of being an agent for change, or "helping people help themselves," to quote the World Bank's mission statement. It is one that runs through all forms of assistance. Being at once an agent of change, an external catalyst of empowerment, and a helper who is actually helpful is a subtle matter. If the helping hand is too heavy, the agent for change can spoil, distort, or suppress initiatives for and commitment to change.

In offering development advice to a country, one should not employ, implicitly or explicitly, a monolithic model of the country and its polity; there are always contending groups with differing views, agendas, and interests. An international development agency should, as much as possible, resist the temptation to take sides in domestic politics. It should offer a range of ideas and good examples, lay out, as scientifically as possible, the evidence, and outline the rationales and the costs of the various options. Intellectually self-confident decisionmakers may ask for our opinion, and we have an obligation to deliver it, professionally and clearly. A country can be "in the driver's seat" and still look for advice from those who are experienced, impartial, and committed to poverty reduction. Local politics may prevent leaders from acknowledging the help, but it is nevertheless generally welcome.

As private capital flows have increased and economies have grown, the IFIs' resources have become still more concentrated on activities that push the boundaries on both the investment climate and governance fronts and on projects with powerful demonstration effects. In each case, precisely because the orientation toward expanding the frontier is of the essence, careful analysis and preparation are vital. Hence the ever-increasing importance of the Bank's analytical work, both in support of broad diagnostic analysis of countries and sectors and in the preparation of individual projects. The growing importance of the "frontier" dimension of our work implies ever-stronger emphasis on the Bank as an ideas or knowledge institution, and thus on research.

The political economy of assistance to reform is a complex art. The agent for change gains skill by learning from others through case studies, "war stories," and apprenticeship, as well as through reflection. Instead of trying to discover or impose a fixed sequence or time path, the agent for change must be open to supporting travel on a number of possible roads. Research on this topic should not search for a blueprint but should seek a "description" of the local landscape so that dead-end paths and pitfalls can be avoided and so that we can give encouragement in the general direction of the more promising paths to reform.

The effectiveness of the IFI as an adviser and agent of change is based on an open, respectful, and long-term relationship with both low-income and middle-income countries. If the IFI is asking a country to be open to new learning and experimentation, it should ask the same of itself. There is no expert quick fix for the problems of social change; there is no royal road to learning what works in a country; and there is no instantaneous solution or cheap shortcut to institutional development. To be an effective agent of change, the IFI must have a relationship with the country that is a genuine partnership and that is based on an understanding of local conditions. Because such understanding requires local presence, the research to build it should eventually be generated as much as possible by the knowledge institutions of the country itself.

The concept of partnership applies to middle-income countries as well as to low-income countries. If we take seriously the common humanity that binds us all, we must recognize that the existence of significant absolute poverty in a middle-income country such as Brazil should not be seen solely as Brazil's problem. To be sure, as a country grows into the ranks of the middle-income countries, our partnership should mature and change. The access to capital markets that comes with rising income opens new opportunities. But while middle-income countries and other emerging markets do gain access to international private capital flows, that access is intermittent, often at arm's length, and sometimes very costly. By contrast, what the IFIs can provide is a steady, responsive partnership and a steady and flexible flow of capital in support of needed reforms. The fight for poverty reduction is a long haul, and the partnership is of special importance when the situation is at its most difficult.

Let me close this discussion on IFIs as agents of change with a word or two to the theorists. Being an effective agent of change requires some understanding of the dynamic process being influenced. There are a number of interesting theoretical questions. First, we have to have some notion of how to convince and encourage. In part, that can be done through information and incentives, for which we have a fairly standard economic theory. But some of the convincing, and I think in development much of it, has to do with changing preferences. Second, we have to think about how to act as an external player in a repeated game if we are to understand how to influence outcomes, especially when the domestic polity is divided. We have to recognize, too, that the external role inevitably becomes internal to the game. Third, it would be good to know whether we should be using a model with high and low equilibria (where a fairly vulgar shove in roughly the right direction might achieve the desired result) or whether we should be using some more complex dynamic model, either equilibrium or disequilibrium. When we try to model explicitly, there is always a danger that some misguided or simplistic clot will take us too literally. But this is a risk that theorists always have to run, and one that is well worth running if we can gain greater insight into these issues.

Conclusion

I have laid out a strategy for development, one based on the twin pillars of investment climate and empowerment. What are the prospects that developing countries will implement this strategy and that the industrial world will provide real support for it? My answer is more positive than it might have been even a few years ago. One cause for hope is the significant improvement in the quality of macroeconomic and trade policies in many developing countries. I have already mentioned the examples of some high-profile reformers, but the phenomenon is more general. For the developing world as a whole, many of the policies that make a difference in growth and poverty alleviation—such as controlling inflation and lowering trade barriers—are better than ever before. For this reason, notwithstanding the recent slowdown in the United States and the continued economic troubles in Japan, we believe that the medium-term outlook for the developing countries is stronger than it has been in many years.

Reforms in the developing world thus create opportunities. But are the rich countries ready to do their part to help countries seize those opportunities? Again, recent trends have strengthened the grounds for optimism.

First, consider trade policy. The returns to improving the investment climate depend in significant part on whether reforming countries have access to foreign markets for their goods. Rich-country barriers in key industries and sectors, such as agriculture and textiles, discourage reforms in the investment climate. But recent movements to increase developing country access—such as the European Union's notably the Everything But Arms initiative, which eliminates all barriers on imports from the very poorest countries—are cause for hope that the rich countries have recognized their responsibility.

Second, the rich countries have increasingly shown that they recognize the need to reduce the administrative burden of aid on developing countries. One of the best ways to move in this direction would be for all countries to follow the lead of the United Kingdom by dropping the practice of tying aid; another is to improve donor coordination.

Third, the most recent data show that there has been a small increase in aid volumes in a number of countries (although in aggregate, the share is still declining).

Finally, both industrial and developing countries have declared their commitment to the International Development Goals for progress against poverty over the next decade and a half. Together, these recent trends signal significant movement toward support for more rapid poverty reduction.

Thus, those making political decisions and formulating economic policies have generated real opportunities for the IFIs to help accelerate development and poverty reduction. Research has a vital role to play in helping to take advantage of those opportunities. We have learned much about what works and what does not work in economic development. We have learned much, too, in recent years about how to catalyze and support reforms most effectively. We have already begun to build this knowledge into our work. There remains, however, much that we still have to learn about the investment climate and empowerment and about how to foster change.

What I have described is, in many ways, only a structuring of the agenda. Our work should build on the understanding of the two-pillar approach that itself has emerged from the research of the past few years. Of course, we have to act on policy in real time; we cannot afford Hamlet's agonized approach to decisionmaking. But today's research underpins tomorrow's crucial decisions. The research agenda I have tried to describe is not only one of deep intellectual challenge and fascination; it can also yield powerful returns in our common fight against poverty.

Investment and Poverty: The Role of the International Financial Institutions

Nicholas Stern

The Jacques de Larosière Lecture
Annual Meeting, The European Bank for Reconstruction
and Development, London, April 22, 2001

It is a special pleasure to be back among friends and colleagues. The European Bank for Reconstruction and Development (EBRD) is a unique institution with an inspiring and challenging mandate. I look back on the six years I spent with you as a most productive and cheerful period of my working life. And it is a great honor to give a lecture bearing the name of Jacques de Larosière. Like many of you, I learned enormously from him and owe him an immense debt. And even as bankers, we must recognize that there are some debts that it is a privilege to bear. Jacques is a very special figure in the international community. He is someone who, through his outstanding abilities, personality, dedication, and charm, has changed the shape of development and progress in the global economy of the past 50 years. Being here today means a great deal to me, and I would like to thank Jean Lemierre, the President of the EBRD, and the Executive Committee of the EBRD for the invitation.

The Issues

My subject is investment and poverty and, in particular, the role of the international financial institutions (IFIs) in promoting the one and overcoming the other. It will be helpful to look first at the basic philosophies and approaches of our two institutions, the World Bank and the EBRD.

The World Bank's *objective* is to fight to overcome poverty in client countries. An increasing proportion of its total lending is in the form of programmatic loans to governments, designed to support change in the economy as a whole or in a major sector. The EBRD's *objective* is to pro-

I would like to thank David Ellerman, Halsey Rogers, and Hans Peter Lankes for their help in preparing this lecture.

mote transition to a market economy. It invests mostly in the private sector, largely through the financing of projects.

The World Bank's development *strategy* (elaborated in chapter 7) stands on two broad pillars: building an investment climate for investment and growth, and empowering poor people to participate in growth. The EBRD's *strategy* focuses on the transition impact of its individual projects and its overall portfolio.

Both institutions must operate according to sound banking principles (although we might have slightly different perceptions of what constitutes sound banking), and both should work to extend the boundaries of what the private sector can do or is willing to do. Of course, pushing out frontiers often involves what economists call externalities—benefits to others for which you are not rewarded. It also often involves taking risks beyond those that private sector market participants will accept. For these reasons, the role of pushing out frontiers requires a public institution.

This lecture will examine the key links between the investment climate and poverty reduction. I will argue that a combination of the philosophies and approaches to development embodied in these two international banks, the EBRD and the World Bank, can give a powerful boost to pro-poor growth. I will make the case that an activist approach by public institutions can help promote a dynamic form of capitalist system that yields strong benefits for poor people. Indeed, these benefits may go far beyond those likely to be achieved by a public policy that attempts to be purely permissive or passive toward private sector development.

We have to see our two international financial institutions as **agents of change.** In a world where the IFIs now represent a relatively small share of international capital flows it is this role, rather than resource transfer, which becomes their primary raison d'être. From this perspective the task of the IFI is to provide funding to *help meet the costs of change and not to meet the costs of not changing.*

The change we work to promote should be to foster pro-poor growth based on the two pillars described above. Thus our approach must be to assist countries to improve the environment for the private sector by promoting good macroeconomic policies, good governance and strong institutions, and the building of the infrastructure necessary to support economic activity—while also participating directly in that economic activity through demonstration projects that push out frontiers.

Lest I be misunderstood, this focus on the "investment climate" does not imply a narrowly pro-big-business view. Rather, the guiding principle of our efforts to foster a good investment climate must be to improve the productivity of all firms, including, notably, farming households and small and medium-size enterprises (SMEs). The goal is increase the well-being of the society as a whole, especially its poor.

I am emphasizing the private sector because it is not only the main engine of aggregate growth but also the main provider of economic activity for poor people. Yet poor people often face enormous obstacles in realizing economic opportunities. And there are many more dimensions of poverty beyond the lack of income associated with the lack of economic opportunity. For both these reasons, an attack on poverty is vastly more successful if, in addition to encouraging economic growth and development, it also focuses on empowering poor people to shape their own lives, through opportunities for education, health care, and participation in the key decisions that affect them and their families. Accordingly, my emphasis here will be, first, on growth driven by the private sector and, second, on how to empower poor people so that they can participate actively in the process of growth. Both elements are crucial for fighting poverty. [*Note to reader: The full version of this lecture provides an elaboration of the strategy and its foundations. In this book these are available in the preceding chapter.*] The main purposed of this lecture is to analyze how, through their lending instruments and in other ways based on their comparative advantages, the IFIs can act in a way that promotes the type of change indicated by a strategy based on these two elements.

As plausible—even obvious—as this strategy for development may sound, it is fairly new and is not universally accepted. But it builds on the intellectual capital bequeathed by development pioneers—those pioneers who, to paraphrase Dante's description of Virgil in his *Purgatory*, "walked at night, carrying the lantern behind, of no help to themselves but illuminating those who follow." Indeed, many of the arguments that I will advance here are based on those that Jacques de Larosière developed and championed in his own way during his time at the French Treasury, the International Monetary Fund (IMF), the Banque de France, and the EBRD. He has always pretended that he is neither an economist nor a philosopher, but those of us who love those subjects and see them as fundamental agents of change have always known that he is both.

Analyzing the Investment Climate

The new emphasis on the investment climate shows how our institutions' two approaches to lending—the transition impact approach championed by the EBRD and what I might call the governance approach of the World Bank—are closely intertwined and mutually supportive. But is it possible to be analytical in assessing or measuring the investment climate? It is, and researchers at both the EBRD and the World Bank have already gone a long way toward doing so. We are helping our clients develop the skills to evaluate the quality of the investment climate in their own countries through systematic surveys of private firms, with a particular focus on small and medium-size enterprises. This research has already demonstrated quite dramatically that a hostile investment climate hits SMEs the hardest.

An important example of this work, and of collaboration between our institutions, is the Business Environment and Enterprise Performance Survey, led by the EBRD. The survey, which polled nearly 4,000 firms in 22 transition countries, broke new ground in quantifying the negative impact of different forms of corruption on the performance of firms. Such surveys are a powerful tool for shedding light on the day-to-day obstacles that domestic firms, not just foreign investors, face in running a business.

Another study in which the World Bank was involved, this one in India, exposed the links between poor infrastructure, onerous bureaucracies, low growth, and slow progress in reducing poverty. Among the 10 Indian states included in the survey, those with a more favorable investment climate were also doing better in the fight against poverty.

Also important for our understanding is the hands-on experience that the IFIs have gained in their development work. Channels for systematically gathering and transmitting this experience include organizations such as the Foreign Investment Advisory Councils, in which the EBRD has played a strong role, and similar activities by the World Bank Group in many countries. The EBRD has long recognized that it can affect the transition process not only through the transition impact of its projects but also by working with governments to understand, and thereby influence, the investment climate.

These various types of information complement each other and will enable the IFIs to support clients, both inside and outside the government, in analyzing the impediments to investment and the costs of those impediments. We are likely to discover that in one country petty corruption is the primary problem, in another, unreliable power, and in a third, transport infrastructure, while in a fourth the challenge is to promote a free press and civil society that can expose grand corruption. In this way, a good diagnostic survey can be a filter through which we look at different possible interventions, establish priorities, and relate our activities to what other IFIs are doing.

The Role of the IFIs in the Age of Globalization

The new international financial architecture marks one of the most radical changes in the past decade or so. It has brought massive increases both in trade and private capital flows, along with exchange-rate volatility and greater pressure for sound economic policies. To use language that has become current, and often emotionally charged, there has been a remarkable acceleration in the pace of globalization.

Different people mean different things by globalization. What I mean by it is the growing integration of economies and societies through the cross-country flows of information, ideas, activities, technologies, goods, services, capital, and people. The past decade has seen extraordinary changes, particularly in communications technologies. We are also seeing declines in transport costs, more open policies toward international trade and movement of capital, and striking increases in world trade volumes and capital flows. The result is a much more integrated world economy than we had just 10 years ago.

Those of us who work in the IFIs are keenly aware of the changes and pressures that the acceleration of globalization brings for our institutions. In fact, Jacques de Larosière discussed the role of the IFIs in a world of private capital flows five years ago in his Per Jacobsson Lecture at the 1996 Bank-Fund Annual Meetings. I can only add a few thoughts to his main points.

I will argue, with Jacques de Larosière, that the IFIs do continue to have a role but that it is a changed role. The IFIs now start unavoidably from the premise that the private sector is the engine or locomotive of growth and development; surely the failures of developmental dirigisme and the collapse of command economies have taught us that lesson. It is central to the role of the IFIs, therefore, to promote and foster private sector–driven growth—and to do so in ways that are pro-poor.

It is worth spending a moment to elaborate on this point. The IFIs, as promoters of development, should work to *create new opportunities*. This way of stating the objective has at least two implications. First, it means that development assistance should facilitate private investment—for example, through building a sound regulatory environment or upgrading the skills of the labor force—rather than substitute for such investment. Second, development assistance must be designed in such a way as to help build and increase the productivity of public resources rather than merely replace such resources. To achieve these goals, the IFIs must succeed in helping countries improve the investment climate, on the one hand, and must support country ownership of and commitment to reform initiatives, on the other. To push the metaphor, if the private sector is the locomotive of development, the IFIs' role is to help countries lay track and create railway networks. Moreover, the IFIs need to do so in a way that encourages the country to invest in improving systems and to build sound additional rail lines on its own, rather than simply rely on engineering and financing provided by the IFIs. If we want to strain the metaphor still further, there may also be moments when the IFIs can help to push-start a stalled locomotive.

New Perspectives on Lending

What instruments are best suited to this approach? How can the IFIs structure their lending programs so that they help fund the costs of changing rather than the costs of not changing? On the lending side, we at the World Bank are moving toward a *programmatic approach*—that is, toward programs that cover a substantial part of the economy, involve basic policy reforms, and operate with multiyear financing. These may be investments that involve substantial support for a sector or area of activity, or they may be programs for economywide adjustment. Within this approach, we will make use of two major lending instruments: programmatic adjustment lending and programmatic investment lending.

Programmatic adjustment lending. The aim of programmatic adjustment lending is to meet the costs of reforming rather than to cover the costs of not reforming. Its key role is to support reforms that are oriented toward growth and poverty reduction by helping to meet the up-front costs of adjustment. Where country circumstances permit, the World Bank will increasingly provide aid in this form. These loans are policy- and performance-based budget support loans, without the strong process-based conditionality of traditional adjustment lending—and without the negative connotations of "adjustment" as a response to past failures. Such lending is a powerful vehicle for backing serious reforms in countries that have or are establishing good track records. Twenty years of experience with adjustment and other programmatic lending suggests that this type of support is most effective when it is grounded in strong borrower commitment to reform and disbursed on the basis of actions on the ground, rather than promises. In these circumstances, budgetary support can be a particularly effective vehicle for assisting reform.

Programmatic lending has an advantage over project-based lending as a means of supporting reform in that it promotes *greater ownership* of development strategies by the borrowing country. Borrower commitment to reform is likely to depend on the degree of autonomy that the country has in setting out its own development strategy, building on its knowledge and understanding of the local situation. Because countries are able to reflect their priorities better within the larger program than within a project, the programmatic approach can increase country ownership. Of course, an IFI with a mandate to fight poverty cannot support a program merely on the grounds that it is "country-owned"; it must also be convinced that the program will be effective in reducing poverty.

Programmatic investment lending. The programmatic approach is not limited to budgetary support for economywide or sectorwide adjustment and development. It also applies to projects that are of such scope and influence that they take on many of the characteristics of sectorwide adjustment programs. Let me mention just two leading examples from our portfolio that I have had the privilege of witnessing firsthand in recent months. One is the District Primary Education Programme in India, which encompasses over 50 million students and is thus large in relation to educational "projects" in the traditional sense. The second is the Kecamatan Development Program in Indonesia, which in many regions provides block grants to support village-level projects throughout the country. The India project has dramatically changed how communities are involved in education and how girls benefit from education. The Indonesia project is a powerful example of how communities can be empowered to allocate public resources.

Demonstration projects. Complementing these programmatic instruments will be a greater emphasis by the World Bank on demonstration projects. Even with the shift to increased use of budgetary support and sectorwide program lending, project lending will remain a powerful tool for Bank assistance to borrower countries. The difference is that projects will now be used where they are most effective—in demonstrating the value of new approaches and in building capacity. The stakes in development are too high, and the resources too limited, to allow us to carry out what might be called "enclave projects" that may have a positive effect within the confines of the project but that lead neither to significant knowledge spillovers nor to the building of capacity for the future. Indeed, if not carefully designed with fungibility concerns in mind, IFI efforts may simply displace the country's own earlier initiatives, so that in the end the IFI projects may have minimal net developmental effect. For example, if an IFI lends to a country without promoting change that could promote its own ability to raise resources or its creditworthiness it may simply have the effect of displacing another project and reducing the creditworthiness from other sources.

By contrast, demonstration projects not only have a significant direct effect but also spark similar reforms throughout an economy. The EBRD has been in the lead in developing the theory and practice of demonstration projects as a participant-investor. It has shown that an IFI can provide serious analysis and measurement that can guide project selection and strategic decisions. In the EBRD's terminology, the desired outcome is "transition impact." The analogous term in the language of the International Finance Corporation (IFC) is "development impact." Both the EBRD and the IFC have done much to prove the value of demonstration projects by pioneering new approaches and exploring new markets, thus lighting the way for further private sector initiatives. It is not for me to pick out the outstanding EBRD examples, but I do remember the municipal utility projects in Central Europe, the equity invested in private banks in Bosnia just one year after the Dayton Peace Accords, and the trade facilitation program first developed in Russia in 1995. Obviously, if the IFIs are taking the risks that they should, not every project will be a success, let alone have spillover effects. Nevertheless, every proposed project should be judged against the criterion of its potential for spillovers.

These demonstration effects can apply across countries, as well as across jurisdictions within a country. Indeed, one advantage of the IFIs is their ability to help propagate such spillovers. A recent example is the market-based land reforms in northeast Brazil, which have been implemented successfully in several states with World Bank support and are now being replicated throughout Brazil's poorer states. This is, in fact, a good example of *international* demonstration effects, since the original model came from South Africa and the Brazilian program is now being emulated by other countries, including Guatemala and the Philippines. Similarly, with World Bank support the Indian state of Karnataka is about to launch a state-level value added tax (VAT) that will both establish a buoyant revenue base and, over time, reduce administrative harassment. Karnataka's example is likely to be followed by other states in India.

The IFIs' Comparative Advantage

The IFI's lending instruments are not the only instruments available for IFIs to generate change that can promote growth and poverty reduction. Indeed these instruments—programmatic adjustment lending, programmatic investment lending, and demonstration projects—are most effective when combined with other assets and tools which are at the disposal of the IFIs and which embody their comparative advantage relative to most other financial or development institutions. They include:

- Extensive knowledge about what development approaches are effective in what circumstances, bred of cross-country experience and serious research

- A financial structure that is well suited to managing the risks and challenges inherent in development assistance

- A concern for capacity building, together with instruments for promoting it

- An ability to use well-designed conditionality to help countries commit to reforms

- An ability to serve as a "convener" of the international community around pressing development issues

These characteristics of IFIs help answer two obvious questions about the IFIs and the private sector. How can the IFIs partner with the private sector so that the latter can do what it could not otherwise do? Why cannot capital markets do the job of institutional reform and economic development?

I have already touched on the IFIs' research and information-sharing programs. Let me elaborate here on the last four points.

Institutional structure and risk management. Some pioneering development projects would be within the ambit of private investment were it not for the great commercial, social, and political risks that often accompany innovation in developing countries. The IFIs' capital structures allow them to absorb part of these risks in partnership with private investment. Moreover, the relationship IFIs have with governments enables them to reduce political risks in ways that a private investor could not. First-time foreign investors may make an investment that they would otherwise avoid if they can rely on the prior knowledge, experience, relationships, and standing that an IFI has in the country. Finally, the IFIs can bring local project development experience to new private investors to help projects get off the ground.

How do we ensure that this support does not become a crutch? How can IFI assistance enable new private sector activity without creating an en-feebling dependency on international subsidies? This question goes to the heart of the current debate about the IFIs. Critics might argue that investors love to fill the holes in their otherwise unfundable projects with pub-lic monies and that this distorts rather than strengthens market discipline. Similarly, investors would welcome the IFIs' running their interference for them with the political authorities, but that would postpone the day when the rights of private entrepreneurship and investment will be respected. These are serious arguments that the IFIs must take to heart.

Capacity building. The answer lies in the developmental learning and demonstration effect. The involvement of an IFI is premised on the idea that, ultimately, the learning and capacity building it brings about will render its involvement unnecessary. In this sense, the job of an IFI is to continually work itself out of a job, assisting countries to increase their capacity to carry out development reforms and, gradually, to replace the IFI's technical expertise with their own. In doing so, an IFI has to em-body the impartiality implied by its public and international status. It has to work to improve the investment climate for all investors, small and large, domestic and foreign, and not just for its current clients.

This answer speaks to the whole issue of the role of the IFIs in a world of globalized private capital flows. The capacity-building business of a public development institution is fundamentally different from that of a private business. Imagine a country that needs to build 10 power plants at reasonable prices. For a commercial institution, repeat business is the firm's business; the incentive is to build the first power plant in such a way that the country's government then commits to purchase the other nine plants from the same supplier. By contrast, our role as IFIs is to ensure that the country's government and domestic suppliers develop the managerial and technical capacity to build and operate the needed power infrastructure cost-effectively. Our interest is not in building power plants for their own sake but in putting the country in charge of the process of analyzing its own needs and meeting its own development goals. Therefore, our involvement should be geared toward building one power plant as a demonstration project while helping the country develop the institutional structure that will promote the construction and management of the other nine plants.

We should yield to no one in recognizing the promise of international private capital flows for growth and development. But we should with equal force assert the distinctive role of the IFIs: to assist client countries in fostering the institutional learning and the improvement of the investment climate that are necessary to design their own development successes, and to help ensure that the poor within those countries share in that great promise.

Conditionality. There will be moments when, in pursuit of the goal of poverty reduction, the IFI has to take a chance and support a serious reform program that is under threat. Here is where conditionality can be effective. A reformer who is trying to limit the effectiveness of the opposition to reform measures may seek conditionality as a way of tying a country more closely into the reforms. Such support has to be supplied judiciously. We have to be aware that it can backfire and that it may be ineffective where divisions are too deep. We have to be realistic and to assess whether the program, even with our support, has a chance of success. Conditionality is no substitute for real commitment to reform. But I have no doubt—and we often hear it from reforming ministers who quietly ask for conditionality on key issues—that it can be a substantial help at crucial times in taking reforms forward.

The IFIs can help to strengthen and broaden reform coalitions: Reform A might be, with the help of IFIs, be recast in a form that would be more complementary and conducive to Reform B, inducing the beneficiaries of Reform B to join the coalition. Conditionalities backed by resources can play a similar role in helping to build a reform coalition. The IFI-supplied resources might also cover the costs of adjustments required by the reform, bringing on board some who might otherwise be in opposition. Eventually, the reform coalition might be broad enough to reach the tipping point so that even indifferent bystanders would want to join the winning team. By anticipating problems, by being creative in suggesting possible solutions, and by adding its integrity in support, the IFI can help foster a "deal for reform" that might not otherwise materialize. If its integrity is to be maintained and have a real effect over time, the IFI's support should be focused on programs that have a real chance of success and are likely to benefit poor people.

Convening. Finally, we can see the IFIs, and particularly the World Bank, as having a power of "convening" that arises from their special ownership structure and goals. The World Bank is itself a big coalition of countries, and it is devoted to the overarching goal of poverty reduction. The convening power is unique and is a crucial aspect of its ability to act as an agent of change. One current example is the Nile Basin Initiative, which aims to promote development by managing and sharing water resources equitably among the ten Nile Basin countries. The Bank has supported and facilitated the initiative, and at the request of the member countries has coordinated donor support of this cooperative effort. A second example—in this case working within individual borrowing countries—has been the Bank's role in convening donors and promoting coordination through the Poverty Reduction Strategy process.

Conclusion

In conclusion, I would like not only to assert but also to celebrate the distinctive role of the IFIs. Too often, development institutions are seen or portrayed as agencies that think they are solving grand collective action problems but that are actually pursuing rather mundane and parochial ends. Yet such a picture does not tell the real story.

From the ancient Stoics onward, there has been the vision that we are all not merely citizens of our own *polis* but also citizens of the world. There is a lower self that is indelibly marked by the accidents of birth and upbringing, but there is also a higher self that can overlook these particulars to recognize a common humanity. Countries, like individuals, are prone to see issues narrowly in terms of their self-interest, and thus the IFIs are sometimes viewed as simply devices for pursuing the ends of the rich countries that are their dominant shareholders. We all—shareholders, management, and employees—would be selling our mission short if we saw it that way.

The development agencies should be seen as, and act as, institutional mechanisms in which countries contractually pledge themselves to pursue higher ends. In the IFIs each member country is like an Odysseus binding itself to the collective mast of international development and governance. Thus the country commits itself to resist the siren songs of parochial interests in order to pursue that common good. For all its riches and promise, the world community is threatened by poverty and disease. The IFIs must now, more than ever, call on their member nations to go beyond narrow interests and to renew their common com-mitment to the overall development of humankind.

High ideals, however, are not enough. We have to know what we are trying to do, have a strategy, and be effective in influencing that strat-egy. Our responsibility is all the more serious because we now know more than ever about which strategies are most effective in promoting development, as well as what role the IFIs can most usefully play as agents of change. Strategically, we know that we need to focus on im-proving the investment climate and empowering poor people. Opera-tionally, we know that the most effective tools for achieving these reforms are programmatic lending and projects with powerful demon-stration effects, always bound together with the knowledge, capacity building, and mutual commitment that the IFIs can offer.

This knowledge about what works is born from the experience of the EBRD and the World Bank, which have led the way in accumulating the experience and analysis on which our vision is based. The develop-ing world has itself been drawing its lessons, and economic policies have improved markedly over the past 10 years. The result is that, for the first time in decades, per capita income in developing countries is growing more rapidly than in industrial countries. This surge is far from uniform, but on average, it is happening.

Thus, there are more favorable circumstances in the developing world; we have a deeper understanding of development; and we know more about how the IFIs can work most effectively. Our opportunity to make real progress in the fight against poverty has never been greater. To paraphrase Churchill, "We have the tools; let's get on with the job."

References

The word *processed* describes informally reproduced works that may not be commonly available through libraries.

Abramovitz, Moses, and Paul David. 1973. "Reinterpreting Economic Growth: Parables and Realities." *American Economic Review* 63 (2): 428–39.

Acharya, Shanka, and Ashok Mitra. 2000. "The Potential of Rural Industries and Trade to Provide Decent Work Conditions: A Data Reconnaissance in India." SAAT Working Paper. South Asia Multidisciplinary Advisory Team, International Labour Organisation, New Delhi.

Alderman, Harold, and Marito Garcia. 1994. "Food Security and Health Security: Explaining the Levels of Nutritional Status in Pakistan." *Economic Development and Cultural Change* 42 (3): 485–507.

Alderman, Harold, Peter Orazem, and Elizabeth Paterno. 2001. "School Quality, School Cost and the Public/Private School Choices of Low-Income Households in Pakistan." *Journal of Human Resources* 36 (2): 304–26.

Bauer, Peter T. 1972. *Dissent on Development*. Cambridge, Mass.: Harvard University Press.

Becker, Jasper. 2000. *The Chinese*. New York: Free Press.

Behrman, Jere R., and Anil Deolalikar. 1995. "Are There Differential Returns to Schooling by Gender? The Case of Indonesian Labour Markets." *Oxford Bulletin of Economics and Statistics* 57 (February): 97–118.

Bloom, David E., and Jeffrey D. Sachs. 1998. "Geography, Demography, and Economic Growth in Africa." *Brookings Papers on Economic Activity* 0 (2, September): 207–73.

Bruno, Michael, and Hollis B. Chenery. 1962. "Development Alternatives in an Open Economy." *Economic Journal* 72 (285): 79–103.

Burnside, Craig, and David Dollar. 2000. "Aid, Policies, and Growth." *American Economic Review* 90 (4, September): 847–68.

Chen, Shaohua, and Yan Wang. 2001. "China's Growth and Poverty Reduction: Recent Trends between 1990 and 1999." World Bank, Washington, D.C. Processed.

CII (Confederation of Indian Industry). 2000. "From Crumbs to Riches: Re-Orienting Foreign Direct Investment in India." New Delhi.

CII (Confederation of Indian Industry) and World Bank. 2001. "Firm Analysis and Competitiveness Survey of India." New Delhi.

Collier, Paul. 2000. "Ethnicity, Politics, and Economic Performance." *Economics and Politics* 12 (3): 225–45.

Collier, Paul, and Ashish Garg. 1999. "On Kin Groups and Wages in the Ghanaian Labor Market." *Oxford Bulletin of Economics and Statistics* 61 (2): 133–57.

Collier, Paul, and J. W. Gunning. 1999. "Explaining African Economic Performance." *Journal of Economic Literature* 37: 64–111.

Collier, Paul, and Anke Hoeffler. 2000. "Greed and Grievance in Civil War." Policy Research Working Paper 2355. World Bank, Development Research Group, Washington, D.C.

Collier, Paul, Anke Hoeffler, and Catherine Pattillo. 2001. "Flight Capital as a Portfolio Choice." *The World Bank Economic Review* 15 (2): 55–80.

Datt, Gaurav, and Martin Ravallion. 1998a. "Farm Productivity and Rural Poverty in India." *Journal of Development Studies* 34: 62–85.

———. 1998b. "Why Have Some Indian States Done Better than Others at Reducing Rural Poverty?" *Economica* 65: 17–38.

Diamond, Peter, and James A. Mirrlees. 1971a. Optimal Taxation and Public Production I: Production Efficiency. *The American Economic Review* 61(1): 8–27.

———. 1971b. Optimal Taxation and Public Production II: Tax Rules. *The American Economic Review* 61(3): 261–78.

Diwan, Ishac, and Lyn Squire. 1995. "Private Assets and Public Debts: External Finance in a Peaceful Middle East." *Middle East Journal* 49 (winter): 69–88.

Dollar, David, and Roberta Gatti. 1999. "Gender Inequality, Income, and Growth: Are Good Times Good for Women?" Background paper for *Engendering Development*. World Bank, Washington, D.C.

Dollar, David, and Aart Kraay. 2001. "Growth Is Good for the Poor." Policy Research Working Paper 2587. World Bank, Development Research Group, Washington, D.C.

Dollar, David, and Jakob Svensson. 2000. "What Explains the Success or Failure of Structural Adjustment Programs?" *Economic Journal* 466: 894–917.

Dollar, David, Raymond Fisman, and Roberta Gatti. Forthcoming. "Are Women Really the 'Fairer' Sex? Corruption and Women in Government." *Journal of Economic Behavior and Organization*.

Drèze, Jean, and Amartya Sen. 1995. *India: Economic Opportunity and Social Development*. New Delhi: Oxford University Press.

————. Forthcoming. *India: Economic Development and Social Opportunity*. 2nd ed. New Delhi: Oxford University Press.

Easterly, William. 2000. "The Lost Decades . . . and the Coming Boom? Policies, Shocks, and Developing Countries' Stagnation, 1980–1998." World Bank, Washington, D.C. Processed.

————. 2001. "Pakistan's Critical Constraint: Not the Financing Gap but the Social Gap." World Bank, Washington, D.C. Processed.

Easterly, William, and Ross Levine. 1997. "Africa's Growth Tragedy: Policies and Ethnic Divisions." *Quarterly Journal of Economics* 112 (4): 1203–50.

Easterly, William, Norman Loayza, and Peter Montiel. 1997. "Has Latin America's Post-Reform Growth Been Disappointing?" *Journal of International Economics* 43: 287–311.

Elbadawi, Ibrahim, and Nicholas Sambanis. Forthcoming. "How Much War Will We See? Estimating the Incidence of Civil War in 161 Countries." *Journal of Conflict Resolution*.

Gazdar, Haris. 2000. "State, Community, and Universal Education: A Political Economy of Public Schooling in Rural Pakistan." October. Asia Research Centre, London School of Economics.

Haberler, Gottfried, and Anthony Y. C. Koo. 1985. *Selected Essays of Gottfried Haberler*. Cambridge, Mass.: MIT Press.

Hallward-Driemeier, Mary. 2001. "Firm-Level Survey Provides Data on Asia's Corporate Crisis and Recovery." Policy Research Working Paper 2515. World Bank, Washington, D.C.

Hayek, Friedrich A., von. 1984. *Money, Capital, and Fluctuations: Early Essays*. Chicago, Ill.: University of Chicago Press.

Hirschman, Albert O. 1958. *The Strategy of Economic Development*. New Haven, Conn.: Yale University Press.

Hussain, Athar, Nicholas Stern, and Joseph Stiglitz. 2000. "Chinese Reforms from a Comparative Perspective." In Peter J. Hammond and Gareth Myles, eds., *Incentives, Organization, and Public Economics: Papers in Honour of Sir James Mirrlees*. New York: Oxford University Press.

International Institute for Management Development. 2000. *The World Competitiveness Yearbook 2000*. Lausanne.

Israel, Arturo. 1987. *Institutional Development: Incentives to Performance*. Baltimore, Md.: Johns Hopkins University Press.

Jalan, Jyotsna, and Martin Ravallion. 1998a. "Are There Dynamic Gains from a Poor-Area Development Program?" *Journal of Public Economics* 67: 65–85.

———. 1998b. "Transient Poverty in Post-Reform Rural China." *Journal of Comparative Economics* 26: 338–57.

———. 1999. "Are the Poor Less Well Insured? Evidence on Vulnerability to Income Risk in Rural China." *Journal of Development Economics* 58(1): 61–82.

———. 2000. "Geographic Poverty Traps? A Micro Model of Consumption Growth in Rural China." World Bank, Washington, D.C. Processed.

———. Forthcoming. "Behavioral Responses to Risk in Rural China." *Journal of Development Economics*.

Jimenez, Emmanuel, and Yasuyuki Sawada. 1999. "Do Community-Managed Schools Work? An Evaluation of El Salvador's EDUCO Program." *The World Bank Economic Review* 13 (3): 415–41.

Kaufmann, Daniel, Aart Kraay, and Pablo Zoido-Lobatón. 1999a. "Aggregating Governance Indicators." Working Paper. World Bank Institute, Washington, D.C.

———. 1999b. "Governance Matters." Policy Research Working Paper 2196. World Bank, Development Research Group and World Bank Institute, Washington, D.C.

Kim, Jooseop, Harold Alderman, and Peter Orazem. 1998. "Can Cultural Barriers Be Overcome in Girls' Schooling? The Community Support Program in Rural Balochistan." Working Paper Series on Impact Evaluation of Education Reforms 10. World Bank, Development Research Group, Washington, D.C.

———. 1999. "Can Private School Subsidies Increase Schooling for the Poor? The Quetta Urban Fellowship Program." *The World Bank Economic Review* 13 (3): 443–65.

King, Elizabeth, Peter Orazem, and Elizabeth Paterno. 1999. "Promotion with and without Learning: Effects on Student Dropout." Working Paper Series on Impact Evaluation of Education Reforms 18. World Bank, Development Research Group, Washington, D.C.

King, Elizabeth, Peter Orazem, and Darin Wohlgemuth. 1999. "Central Mandates and Local Incentives: The Colombia Education Voucher Program." *The World Bank Economic Review* 13 (3): 467–91.

Klasen, Stephan. 1999. "Does Gender Inequality Reduce Growth and Development? Evidence from Cross-Country Regressions." Background paper for *Engendering Development*. World Bank, Washington, D.C.

Kornai, Janos. 1990. *The Road to a Free Economy. Shifting from a Socialist System: The Example of Hungary*. New York: Norton.

Kravis, Irving B., Alan W. Heston, and Robert Summers. 1982. *World Product and Income: International Comparisons of Real Gross Product*. Baltimore, Md.: Johns Hopkins University Press.

Krugman, Paul. 1995. "Dutch Tulips and Emerging Markets." *Foreign Affairs* 74 (4, July/August): 28–44.

Kuznets, Simon. 1971. *Economic Growth of Nations: Total Output and Production Structure*. Cambridge, Mass.: Harvard University Press.

Lanjouw, Peter, and A. Shariff. 2000. "Rural Non-Farm Employment in India: Access, Incomes and Poverty Impact." World Bank, DECRG, Washington, D.C. Processed.

Lanjouw, Peter, and Nicholas Stern, eds. 1998. *Economic Development in Palanpur over Five Decades*. Oxford, U.K.: Oxford University Press.

Lardy, Nicholas. 2001. "Integrating China in the Global Economy." Brookings Institution, Washington, D.C.

Lele, Uma, Kavita Gandhi, and Madhur Gautum. Forthcoming. "India's Poverty, Agriculture and Social Development in a Global Context: Comparisons with Developing Countries and China." World Bank, Washington, D.C. Processed.

Lewis, W. Arthur. 1954. " Economic Development with Unlimited Supplies of Labour." *Manchester School of Economics and Social Studies* 22 (May): 139–91.

———. 1955. *The Theory of Economic Growth*. Homewood, Ill.: Irwin.

Lin, Justin, Fang Cai, and Zhou Li. 1996. *The China Miracle: Development Strategy and Economic Reform*. Hong Kong, China: Chinese University Press.

Machiavelli, Niccolò. 1940 [1513]. *The Prince and the Discourses*. New York: Random House.

Makdisi, Samir, Zeki Fattah, and Imad Limam. 2000. "Determinants of Growth in the Arab Countries." Paper prepared for the Global Research Project. Available at <http://www.gdnet.org/latestnews/latestnews7.htm>.

Mathur, Ajeet N. 1993. "Industrial Restructuring and the National Renewal Fund." Asia Development Bank, Manila. Processed.

Ministry of Industry, India. 1999. *Secretariat of Industrial Activities Newsletter*. August. New Delhi.

Nabli, Mustapha. 2000. "Leading Macroeconomic Issues in MENA." World Bank, Middle East and North Africa Region, Washington, D.C. Processed.

Narayan, Deepa, and Lant Pritchett. 1999. "Cents and Sociability: Household Income and Social Capital in Rural Tanzania." *Economic Development and Cultural Change* 47 (4): 871–97.

Narayan, Deepa, Raj Patel, Kai Schafft, Anne Rademacher, and Sarah Koch-Schulte. 2000. *Voices of the Poor: Can Anyone Hear Us?* New York: Oxford University Press.

National Bureau of Statistics. 2000. *China Rural Poverty Monitoring Report.* Beijing: China Statistics Press.

Pissarides, Christopher. 2000. "Labor Markets and Economic Growth in the MENA Region." Paper prepared for the Global Research Project. Available at <http://www.gdnet.org/latestnews/latestnews7.htm>.

Prebisch, Raúl. 1950. *The Economic Development of Latin America and Its Principal Problems.* New York: UN Economic Commission for Latin America.

Quisumbing, Agnes R. 1996. "Male-Female Differences in Agricultural Productivity." *World Development* 24 (10): 1579–95.

Ravallion, Martin. Documents available at <http://www.worldbank.org/poverty/data/indiapaper.htm>.

Ravallion, Martin, and Shaohua Chen. 2001. "Measuring Pro-Poor Growth." World Bank, Washington, D.C. Processed.

Ravallion, Martin, and Gaurav Datt. 1999. "When Is Growth Pro-Poor? Evidence from the Diverse Experiences of India's States." Policy Research Working Paper 2263. World Bank, Development Research Group, Washington, D.C.

Reinikka, Ritva. 2001. "Recovery in Service Delivery: Evidence from Schools and Clinics." In Ritva Reinikka and Paul Collier, eds., *Uganda's Recovery: The Role of Farms, Firms, and Government.* Washington, D.C.: World Bank.

Reynal-Querol, Marta. Forthcoming. "Ethnicity, Political Systems and Civil War." *Journal of Conflict Resolution.*

Salehi-Isfahani, Djavad. 2000. "Microeconomics of Growth in MENA: The Role of Households." Paper prepared for the Global Research Project. Available at <http://www.gdnet.org/latestnews/latestnews7.htm>.

Schultz, Theodore W. 1993. *The Economics of Being Poor.* Oxford, U.K.: Blackwell.

Schumpeter, Joseph A. 1962. *Capitalism, Socialism and Democracy.* New York: Harper Torchbooks. Originally published 1942.

Sen, Amartya. 1999. *Development as Freedom.* Oxford, U.K.: Oxford University Press.

Singer, Hans W. 1950. "The Distribution of Gains between Investing and Borrowing Countries." *American Economic Review* 40 (May): 473–85.

Smith, Lisa C., and Lawrence Haddad. 2000. *Overcoming Child Malnutrition in Developing Countries: Past Achievements and Future Choices.* Food, Agriculture, and the Environment Discussion Paper 30. Washington, D.C.: International Food Policy Research Institute.

Srinivasan, T. N. 2000. "Growth, Poverty Reduction and Inequality." Yale University, New Haven, Conn. Processed.

State Statistical Bureau. Various years. *Chinese Statistical Yearbook*. Beijing: China Statistics Publishing House.

Stern, Nicholas. 1972. *An Appraisal of Tea Production on Smallholdings in Kenya*, published by the OECD, Paris.

———. 1989. "The Economics of Development: A Survey." *Economic Journal: The Journal of the Royal Economic Society* 99 (Sept.): 597–685.

———. 1991a. "The Determinants of Growth." *Economic Journal: The Journal of the Royal Economic Society* 101 (Jan.): 122–33.

———. 1991b. "Public Policy and the Economics of Development" (The Alfred Marshall Lecture, Aug. 31, 1990, Lisbon.) *European Economic Review* (Netherlands) 35 (April): 241–71.

———. 1992. *Le Rôle de l'Etat dans le Développement Économique*. Lausanne, Switzerland: Editions Payot Lausanne. (Walras-Pareto Lecture given in Lausanne 1991).

———. 1997. "The World Bank as 'Intellectual Actor.'" In Devesh Kapur, John Lewis, and Richard Webb, eds., *The World Bank: Its First Half Century*. Vol. 2: *Perspectives*. Washington D.C.: Brookings Institution Press.

———. 1998. *Economic Development in Palanpur over Five Decades* (with Peter Lanjouw). New York: Oxford University Press.

———. 2001. "Overcoming Poverty in China." Delivered at Beijing University, June. World Bank, Washington, D.C. Processed.

Summers, Lawrence H. 1992. "Investing in *All* the People." Policy Research Working Paper 905. World Bank, Development Economics, Washington, D.C.

Summers, Robert, and Alan Heston. 1988. "A New Set of International Comparisons of Real Product and Price Levels Estimates for 130 Countries, 1950–1985." *Review of Income and Wealth* 34 (1, March): 1–25.

———. 1991. "The Penn World Table (Mark 5): An Expanded Set of International Comparisons, 1950–1988." *Quarterly Journal of Economics* 106 (2, May): 327–68.

Sutton, John. 2000. "The Indian Machine-Tool Industry: A Benchmarking Study." World Bank, Washington, D.C. Processed.

Swamy, Anand, Young Lee, Steve Knack, and Omar Azfar. 1999. *Gender and Corruption*. IRIS Working Paper 232. College Park, Md.: Center for Institutional Reform and the Informal Sector, University of Maryland.

Van de Walle, Dominique. 2000. "Are Returns to Investment Lower for the Poor? Human and Physical Capital Interactions in Rural Vietnam." Policy Research Working Paper 2425. World Bank, Public Economics, Development Research Group, Washington, D.C.

World Bank. 1996. *Improving Basic Education in Pakistan*. Washington, D.C.

————. 1997a. *Confronting AIDS: Public Priorities in a Global Epidemic.* Policy Research Report. New York: Oxford University Press.

————. 1997b. *World Development Report 1997: The State in a Changing World.* New York: Oxford University Press.

————. 1998. *World Development Report 1998/99: Knowledge for Development.* New York: Oxford University Press.

————. 1999a. *World Development Indicators.* Washington, D.C.

————. 1999b. *World Development Report 1999/2000. Entering the 20th Century: The Changing Development Landscape.* New York: Oxford University Press.

————. 2000a. *Anticorruption in Transition: A Contribution to the Policy Debate.* Washington, D.C.

————. 2000b. *Greening Industry: New Roles for Communities, Markets, and Governments.* Policy Research Report. New York: Oxford University Press.

————. 2000c. *Helping Countries Combat Corruption: Progress at the World Bank since 1997.* Washington, D.C.: World Bank.

————. 2000d. *Reforming Public Institutions and Strengthening Governance.* Washington, D.C.: World Bank.

————. 2000e. *World Development Report 2000/2001: Attacking Poverty.* New York: Oxford University Press.

————. 2001a. *China: Overcoming Rural Poverty.* Washington, D.C.

————. 2001b. *Engendering Development: Through Gender Equality in Rights, Resources, and Voice.* Policy Research Report. New York: Oxford University Press.

————. 2001c. *Finance for Growth: Policy Choices in a Volatile World.* Policy Research Report. New York: Oxford University Press.

————. 2001d. *Global Economic Prospects and the Developing Countries: 2001.* Washington, D.C.

————. 2001e. *World Development Report 2002: Building Institutions for Markets.* New York: Oxford University Press.

World Bank Group. 2000. "The World Business Environment Survey (WBES)." Washington, D.C.